Praise for Robert Frank's *Falling Behind*

"I've been a skeptic. Bob Frank is persistent. He's beginning to convince me."

Thomas C. Schelling, author of The Strategy of Conflict
and 2005 Nobel Laureate in Economics

"In this century, distributional concerns will top the policy agenda. This masterful essay will change how you think about them."

Paul Romer, Stanford University

"The arguments here are powerful and multidisciplinary. The crux is explaining how rising economic inequality causes harm to the middle class. . . . This is a gem of a book."

*Lee S. Friedman, Professor of Public Policy,
University of California, Berkeley*

"In this lively, provocative book filled with memorable new examples, Bob Frank goes beyond his previous work (*Luxury Fever, Winner-Take-All Society,* and *Choosing the Right Pond*) and clarifies that 'falling behind' is a consequence not of envy but rather of the simple fact that a person's evaluation of his own possessions 'depends always and everywhere on context' — an unconscious comparison with his neighbor's possessions or with his own previous possessions."

*Laurence Seidman, Chaplin Tyler Professor of Economics,
University of Delaware*

Falling Behind

THE AARON WILDAVSKY FORUM FOR PUBLIC POLICY

Edited by Lee Friedman

This series is to sustain the intellectual excitement that Aaron Wildavsky created for scholars of public policy everywhere. The ideas in each volume are initially presented and discussed at a public lecture and forum held at the University of California.

AARON WILDAVSKY, 1930–1993

"Your prolific pen has brought real politics to the study of budgeting, to the analysis of myriad public policies, and to the discovery of the values underlying the political cultures by which peoples live. You have improved every institution with which you have been associated, notably Berkeley's Graduate School of Public Policy, which as Founding Dean you quickened with your restless innovative energy. Advocate of freedom, mentor to policy analysts everywhere."

*Yale University, May 1993, from text granting
the honorary degree of Doctor of Social Science*

1. *Missing Persons: A Critique of Personhood in the Social Sciences,* by Mary Douglas and Steven Ney
2. *The Bridge over the Racial Divide: Rising Inequality and Coalition Politics,* by William Julius Wilson
3. *The New Public Management: Improving Research and Policy Dialogue,* by Michael Barzelay
4. *Falling Behind: How Rising Inequality Harms the Middle Class,* by Robert H. Frank

Falling Behind

How Rising Inequality
Harms the Middle Class

Robert H. Frank

UNIVERSITY OF CALIFORNIA PRESS

Berkeley   Los Angeles   London

University of California Press, one of the most distinguished
university presses in the United States, enriches lives around
the world by advancing scholarship in the humanities, social
sciences, and natural sciences. Its activities are supported by
the UC Press Foundation and by philanthropic contribu-
tions from individuals and institutions. For more information, visit www.ucpress.edu.

A Caravan Book
For more information, visit www.caravanbooks.org.

University of California Press
Berkeley and Los Angeles, California

University of California Press, Ltd.
London, England

Library of Congress Cataloging-in-Publication Data
Frank, Robert H.
    Falling behind : how rising inequality harms the middle
class / Robert H. Frank.
        p.   cm.
    Includes bibliographical references and index.
    ISBN-13: 978-0-520-25188-5 (cloth : alk. paper)
    ISBN-10: 0-520-25188-1 (cloth : alk. paper)
    ISBN-13: 978-0-520-25252-3 (pbk. : alk. paper)
    ISBN-10: 0-520-25252-7 (pbk. : alk. paper)
    1. Middle class — United States — Economic conditions.
2. Income distribution — United States.   3. Consumption
(Economics) — United States.   4. Equality — Economic
aspects — United States.   I. Title.
HT690.U6F73   2007
305.5'50973 — dc22   2006026248

Manufactured in the United States of America

16   15   14   13   12   11   10   09   08   07
10   9   8   7   6   5   4   3   2   1

This book is printed on New Leaf EcoBook 50, a 100%
recycled fiber of which 50% is de-inked post-consumer
waste, processed chlorine-free. EcoBook 50 is acid-free and
meets the minimum requirements of ANSI/ASTM D5634–01
(Permanence of Paper).

CONTENTS

PREFACE

The psychiatrist George Ainslie, author of the brilliant book *Picoeconomics*, is one of the most interesting and creative people I have ever had the pleasure to know. He remarked to me one afternoon over coffee that the ultimate scarce resource in life is the willingness of other people to pay attention to us. New technologies are constantly creating opportunities to engage with things rather than people, or to watch others perform on television or on film rather than to interact with them directly.

Ainslie argues that it is a basic human need for other people to engage with you, to pay attention to you, to take you seriously. He forecasts that failure to meet this need will prove the most serious and enduring mental health problem of the future. That's not a happy prospect, of course, but his concerns seem hardly far-fetched.

I therefore count myself incredibly fortunate to have had the opportunity to deliver the Aaron Wildavsky Lecture at the Goldman School of Public Policy at the University of California at

Berkeley. The Wildavsky Forum takes place over two days, with a reception and dinner preceding the main lecture on the first day, and then a lengthy panel discussion about the lecture on the following day. I am mindful of what a luxury it was to have had so many smart and experienced people pay such close attention to what I had to say and respond to it in such focused and energetic ways.

I am grateful, too, to have enjoyed the luxury of being able to write this book after having benefited from their commentary. The insightful remarks of Gene Smolensky, Hal Wilensky, and Gene Bardach led to countless improvements. Most important, they persuaded me of the wisdom of launching the book with a discussion of what, exactly, the concept of *relative deprivation* entails.

As my distinguished commentators pointed out, variants of this concept have been discussed for hundreds, even thousands, of years. So we must ask why the concept has never become a serious player in our intellectual debate. It is repeatedly introduced, and each time, after generating a flurry of discussion, it disappears from sight. Why is that?

The answer, I believe, is that many understand the concept far too narrowly. Most people, my commentators included, understand it to entail envy provoked by comparisons with others in more favorable circumstances. Although that may be true in specific cases, I have become increasingly convinced that relative deprivation actually has little to do with envy. Rather, it is fundamentally about the link between context and evaluation. This is a critical point, because, as I will explain, the contrary belief is what has consigned the concept to marginal status.

No one denies that a car experienced in 1950 as having brisk acceleration would seem sluggish to most drivers today. Similarly, a house of given size is more likely to be viewed as spacious the larger it is relative to other houses in the same local environment. And an effective interview suit is one that compares favorably with those worn by other applicants for the same job. In short, evaluation depends always and everywhere on context.

This observation is completely uncontroversial among behavioral scientists. If I am correct that the link between context and evaluation is what relative deprivation is mostly about, then explanations that ignore relative deprivation must also ignore this important link. This is true of the reigning economic models of consumer behavior, for example, which ignore context completely. These models assume that each person's consumption spending is completely independent of the spending of others.

Future intellectual historians will find this more puzzling than the fact that physicians once prescribed leeches to treat fever. Eighteenth-century doctors, after all, had no way of knowing about the germ theory of disease. But ignorance cannot explain the absence of context from economic models. Even those economists who have not studied the relevant social science literature surely know from their own experience how much context matters.

Evaluation guides choice. So if context shapes evaluation, it must also guide choice. In this book I will argue that many economic choices simply cannot be understood without reference to context. But as the animated discussion that followed my Wildavsky Lecture persuaded me, this argument becomes a lot easier to digest if we first attempt to answer this obvious question: If context is so important, why have economists largely ignored it?

In recent years, I have posed this question to a number of friends and colleagues, both in and out of the profession. One suggested that economists will fully embrace context models once it can be shown conclusively that they track the data better than traditional models. Experience, however, suggests otherwise. A case in point is the history of modern consumption theory, which I will discuss in chapter 7.

Another economist speculated that many of our colleagues fear that taking contextual, or positional, concerns seriously might signal a certain lack of rigor. But as recent work has amply demonstrated, there is no barrier to formalizing models that incorporate such concerns.

Still another economist suggested that the aversion to positional concerns might be rooted in the fact that such concerns undermine economists' celebrated invisible hand theorems, which hold that unregulated markets produce the most efficient possible allocation of resources. I suspect there is something to this. Yet the profession has incorporated numerous other forms of market failure into its arsenal of policy recommendations. Even the most ardent proponents of free markets, for example, are quick to concede a productive role for government intervention to curb pollution when transaction costs are high.

Yet another reason I discovered for the aversion to taking explicit account of the influence of context is that many economists feel that to do so would be to give weight to negative emotions such as envy and jealousy, which they feel merit no consideration in normative analysis. They reject models that incorporate context for the same reason they would reject models that give policy weight to the preferences of sadists.

Society does indeed have a legitimate interest in discouraging envy. We should continue to teach our children not to envy the good fortune of others. But the influence of context stems less from envy than from the fact that many important rewards depend on relative position. As I will explain in chapter 5, for example, the median household must keep pace with community spending on housing or else send its children to below-average schools.

Perhaps even more important, context is the very wellspring of the everyday quality judgments that drive consumer demand. That this point is not widely appreciated first became clear to me during a dinner conversation that took place before a lecture I gave at the University of Chicago several years ago. Three of us were waiting outside a restaurant when the fourth member of our dinner party pulled up behind the wheel of a brand new Lexus sedan. Once we were seated at our table, the Lexus owner's first words to me were that he didn't know or care what kinds of cars his neighbors and colleagues drove. As it happened, I had had numerous conversations with this gentleman over the years and found his statement completely credible.

I asked him why he had chosen the Lexus over the much cheaper, but equally reliable, Toyota sedan from the same manufacturer. He responded that it was the car's quality that had attracted him — things like the look and feel of its interior materials, the sound its doors made on closing, and so on. He mentioned with special pride that the car's engine was so quiet and vibration-free that the owner's manual posted warnings in red letters against attempting to start the car while its engine was already running.

I then asked him what car he had been driving before trading up. I forget what he said, but for the sake of discussion suppose that it was a five-year-old Saab. I asked him how he thought people would have reacted to his Saab if it had been possible to transport it back to the year 1935 in a time capsule. He answered without hesitation that anyone from that era would have been extremely impressed. They would have found the car's acceleration and handling spectacular; its interior materials would have amazed them; and its engine would have seemed unbelievably quiet and vibration-free. His own evaluations of his former car were of course strikingly different on each dimension.

We then discussed what a formal mathematical model of the demand for automobile quality might look like, quickly agreeing that any reasonable one would incorporate an explicit comparison of the car's features with the corresponding features of other cars in the same local environment. Cars whose features scored positively in such comparisons would be seen as having high quality, for which consumers would be willing to pay a premium.

Such a model would be essentially identical to one based on a desire, not to own quality for its own sake, but rather to outdo, or avoid being outdone by, one's friends and neighbors. Yet the subjective impressions conveyed by these two descriptions could hardly be more different. To demand quality for its own sake is to be a discerning buyer. But to wish to outdo one's friends and neighbors is to be a boor, a social moron. To be sure, there are people whose aim is to flaunt their superiority over others. But most of us do our best to avoid such people, and the fact that we succeed most of the time suggests that they are relatively rare.

I noticed that on the heels of this discussion, everyone at the table suddenly took much more interest in talking about the kinds of behavior that are driven by contextual concerns. It was fine to talk about behaviors that result from context-dependent perceptions of quality, but not at all palatable to speak of behaviors that result from envy or a desire to outdo others.

In sum, if relative deprivation is really about context, which shapes perceptions of quality, which in turn drive demand, then it is not a peripheral concept. It applies to virtually every good, including basic goods like food. When a couple goes out to dinner for their anniversary, for example, the thought of feeling superior to their friends and neighbors probably never enters their minds. Their goal is just to share a memorable meal. But a memorable meal is a quintessentially relative concept. It is one that stands out from other meals.

With my dinner conversation in Chicago still fresh in memory, I was careful to emphasize, both during my Wildavsky Lecture and in the roundtable discussion the following day, that concerns about context and relative position have little to do with envy of the rich or a desire to keep up with them. Middle-class families don't look to Donald Trump and worry about what he is spending his money on. Likewise, it's totally irrelevant to most in the middle class that Bill Gates has a 40,000-square-foot mansion on the shore of Lake Washington.

The existence of such houses nonetheless affects the spending behavior of people in the middle. It does so through a chain of local comparisons. To begin with, there are people in Bill Gates's league who are influenced by the fact that he built such a house. Indeed, others who live on Lake Washington now have houses even larger than his. Some have 50,000 square feet of living space, some have 60,000, and at least one has 70,000. And just below these people on the economic ladder, there are others for whom these large houses do matter.

For some, they matter because of envy, to be sure. But others are influenced even if they feel no envy. The mere presence of the larger mansions, for example, may shift some people's perceptions about how big a house one can build without seeming overly ostentatious. Or it may change the way people entertain, making dinner parties for thirty-six guests the norm, rather than parties for twenty-four. Or perhaps because their larger mansions make it possible to do so, those at the top of the economic ladder may begin hosting their daughters' wedding receptions in their homes, rather than in hotels or country clubs. Or perhaps people build bigger houses simply because the larger houses of others make their own houses seem small. In each of these instances, we need not invoke envy to explain people's behavior.

The simple point is that local context matters for a host of reasons, most of which have nothing to do with envy or a desire to feel superior to others. Viewing the phenomenon of relative deprivation in terms of such feelings has consigned it to the periphery. This, I will argue, has been a grand mistake, one that has seriously undermined our ability to reach sensible judgments about economic policy.

CHAPTER ONE

Introduction

Many years ago, I attended a lecture by a philosopher who began his talk with a thought experiment. For me as a listener, that approach worked so well that in the years since I have tried to employ it myself at every opportunity. A recent conversation with a neuroscientist friend shed some light on why this device is often so effective. Different parts of the brain, it seems, specialize in thinking about different things. When we are confronted with a question in a specific domain, blood flows to the relevant part of the brain, priming it to think more effectively about the related ideas to follow.

So I want to begin by asking you to conduct not one but two thought experiments. Each is addressed to that part of your brain that thinks — and, more important, that *cares*, in the most deeply personal way — about inequality. Try as best you can to imagine that you are actually confronting the hypothetical choices I am about to describe.

In each case, you must choose between two worlds that are

identical in every respect except one. The first choice is between World A, in which you will live in a 4,000-square-foot house and others will live in 6,000-square-foot houses; and World B, in which you will live in a 3,000-square-foot house and others in 2,000-square-foot houses. Once you choose, your position on the local housing scale will persist.

According to the standard neoclassical economic model of choice, which holds that utility depends on the absolute amount of consumption, the uniquely correct choice is World A. For if absolute house size is all that matters, A is indeed a better world for all, since everyone has a larger house there than the largest house in World B. The important thing, though, is to focus on how *you* would feel in the two worlds.

In fact, most people say they would pick B, where their absolute house size is smaller but their relative house size is larger. Even those who say they would pick A seem to recognize why someone might be more satisfied with a 3,000-square-foot house in B than with a substantially larger house in A. If that is true for you as well, then you accept the main premise required for the arguments I will present.

In the second thought experiment, your choice is between World C, in which you would have four weeks a year of vacation time and others would have six weeks; and World D, in which you would have two weeks of vacation and others one week. This time most people pick C, choosing greater absolute vacation time at the expense of lower relative vacation time.

I use the term *positional good* to denote goods for which the link between context and evaluation is strongest and the term *nonpositional good* to denote those for which this link is weakest.[1] In terms of the two thought experiments, housing is thus a positional good, vacation time a nonpositional good. The point is not that absolute house size and relative vacation time are of no concern. Rather, it is that positional concerns weigh more heavily in the first domain than in the second.

The argument I will advance in this book can be reduced to four simple propositions.

1. *People care about relative consumption more in some domains than in others.* Or, to put this proposition in more neutral language, context matters more in some domains than in others. The two thought experiments just discussed illustrate this proposition. Although context matters for evaluations of both housing and leisure time, it matters more for evaluations of housing.

2. *Concerns about relative consumption lead to "positional arms races," or expenditure arms races focused on positional goods.* In the context of the two thought experiments, this proposition says that individuals will work longer hours to earn the money that will enable them to buy larger houses, expecting to enjoy the additional satisfaction inherent in owning a relatively large house.

3. *Positional arms races divert resources from nonpositional goods, causing large welfare losses.* When people contemplate working longer hours to buy larger houses, they anticipate additional satisfaction not only from having a larger house in absolute terms, but also from having a larger house in relative terms. For the move to appear attractive, the anticipated sum of these two gains must outweigh the loss in satisfaction associated with having fewer hours of leisure. When all make the same move in

tandem, however, the distribution of relative house size remains essentially as before. So no one experiences the anticipated increase in relative house size. When the dust settles, people discover that the gain in absolute house size alone was insufficient to compensate for the leisure that had to be sacrificed to get it. Yet failure to buy a larger house when others do is not an attractive option for the individual, either. As in the familiar stadium metaphor, all stand to get a better view, but when all stand no one sees better than when all were seated.

Because proposition 3 contradicts standard assertions about efficient resource allocation in competitive markets, the impulse of many economists will be to reject it. Yet its logic is precisely the same as the logic that governs the analogous, and completely uncontroversial, claim regarding military arms races. People in every nation want both a high material standard of living and protection from aggression from other nations. To protect against aggression, resources must be diverted from other forms of consumption into military armaments. Relative expenditures clearly matter more in the armaments domain than in the consumption domain. After all, a nation that spends less than its rivals on armaments puts its political independence at risk, whereas one that spends less than its rivals on consumption risks only a reduction in relative living standards. In short, military arms races result because most people believe that being less well armed than one's rivals is more costly than having fewer flat-panel television sets. By the same token, positional arms races result because consumption evaluations are more sensitive to context in some domains than in others.

4. *For middle-class families, the losses from positional arms races have been made worse by rising inequality.* As I will presently discuss, most of the income gains in the United States during the past several decades have gone to people at the top of the income distribution. Not surprisingly, their higher incomes have led these people to build larger houses. There is little evidence that middle-class families envy the good fortune of the wealthy. Yet through a chain of indirect effects I will describe, the larger houses at the top have led families in the middle to spend sharply higher fractions of their incomes on housing, in the process forcing them to curtail other important categories of spending.

Our task in the pages ahead will be to examine these propositions in greater detail. But before taking up the question of whether rising inequality harms the middle class, I will first examine the extent to which inequalities in income and wealth have, in fact, been rising.

CHAPTER TWO

Recent Changes in Income and Wealth Inequality

Presidential aspirants since Ronald Reagan have urged us to ask whether we're better off now than we were four years ago. At any time from 1945 to the early 1970s, the answer for most Americans would have been a resounding yes. Throughout that period, incomes grew at about 3 percent a year for families up and down the income ladder.

Today, however, this question is more difficult to answer. During the past several decades, the distributions of income and wealth in the United States have changed in such a way that the economic environment for most upper-middle-class people has become much more like that of World A than of World B in our earlier thought experiment. For example, although the top 1 percent of earners now have more than three times as much purchasing power as in 1979, the real earnings of families in the middle have risen only slightly since then. The meager income growth that these families have experienced has come not from hourly wage increases, but rather from growth in the labor force participation of married women.

The conventional wisdom has long been that a growing gap between the rich and the middle class is a bad thing. But that view is now under challenge. Some revisionists, respected economists among them, argue that inequality doesn't really matter so long as no one ends up with less in absolute terms. Using income levels to measure the well-being of individual families, these inequality optimists argue that since the rich now have much more money than before and the middle class doesn't have less, society as a whole must be better off.

Yet "having more income" and "being better off" do not have exactly the same meaning. I will argue that changes in spending patterns prompted by recent changes in the distributions of income and wealth have imposed not only important psychological costs on middle-income families but also a variety of more tangible economic costs.

I begin with a brief look at the changes that have occurred in the distributions of income and wealth in the United States during the decades following World War II. Income growth from 1949 until the end of 1970s was well depicted by the famous picket-fence chart shown in figure 1. Incomes grew at about the same rate for all income classes during that period, a little less than 3 percent per year. It varied a bit across income classes, but no matter where you fell along the income scale, you enjoyed fairly robust income growth.

Since consumption expenditures tend to track incomes closely, spending was also increasing at a fairly uniform rate across the income scale during this period. The houses in which

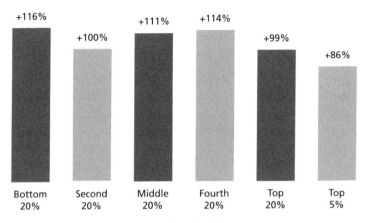

Figure 1. Changes in before-tax household incomes, 1949–1979.
Source: www.census.gov/hhes/income/histinc/fo3.html.

rich people lived in 1979 were bigger than those of their counterparts in 1949, but the same was also true, and by roughly the
same proportion, of the houses in which poor and middle-
income people lived. In short, income and consumption growth
were balanced across income categories during the three decades
following World War II.

That pattern began to change at some point during the 1970s.
Some people date the change even earlier than that. In any event,
if we look at the period from 1979 to 2003, we can see how dramatically different the later income growth pattern is from the
earlier one. In the more recent period, shown in figure 2, people
at the bottom of the income distribution gained only just over 3
percent in real purchasing power terms, and gains throughout
the middle were also very small. For example, median family
earnings were only 12.6 percent higher at the end of that twenty-
four-year period than at the beginning. Income gains for families

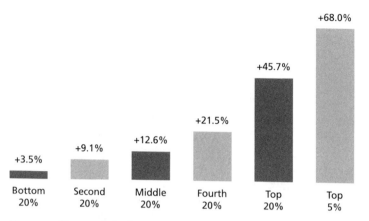

Figure 2. Changes in before-tax incomes, 1979–2003. Source: www.census.gov/hhes/income/histinc/ho3ar.html.

in the top quintile were substantially larger, and larger still for those in the top 5 percent. Yet even for these groups, income growth was not as great as during the earlier period. The later period was thus a time not only of slower growth but also, and more important, of much more uneven growth.

Income inequality has also increased in two important ways not portrayed in figures 1 and 2. One is that changes in the income-tax structure during the presidency of Ronald Reagan significantly shifted real after-tax purchasing power in favor of those atop the socioeconomic ladder. Tax rates on top earners were increased slightly in the final year of the George H. W. Bush administration and further still during the administration of Bill Clinton, which also increased the earned income tax credit for working families with low incomes. But those interim adjustments were far outweighed by the large additional tax cuts targeted toward high-income families by George W. Bush. A sec-

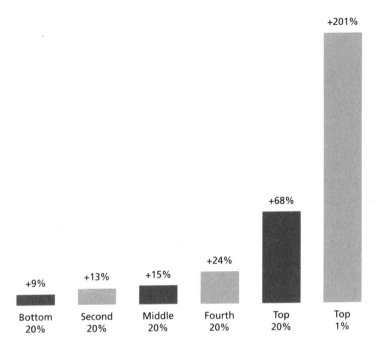

Figure 3. Change in after-tax household income, 1979–2000. Source: Greenstein and Shapiro 2003.

ond change not reflected in figures 1 and 2 is the magnitude of the earnings gains recorded by those at the very top.

Figure 3 portrays some of the results of these two additional effects. Note that the middle 20 percent of earners (net of both tax and transfer payments) gained slightly more ground than in figure 2, which showed pretax incomes (net of transfer payments). Note also that the gains accruing to the top 1 percent in figure 3 are almost three times as large as the corresponding pretax gains experienced by the top 5 percent in figure 2.

Even more spectacular income growth has occurred within

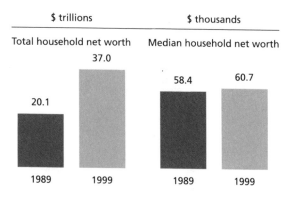

Figure 4. Changes in net worth, 1989–1999. Sources: Wolff 1998; www.inequality.org.

the top 1 percent of earners. Only fragmentary data exist for people that high up in the income distribution, but there are snapshots here and there that show us what has been happening. One valuable source is the salaries of CEOs, which *Business Week* has been tracking for more than twenty years. In 1980, the CEOs of Fortune 200 companies earned about forty-two times as much as the average worker. That ratio had grown to more than five hundred times as much by 2000. And there is evidence that the gains have been even more pronounced for those who stand even higher than CEOs on the income ladder.

A similar picture emerges when we look at how the distribution of wealth has changed over time. In recent years, it has been widely reported that roughly half of all Americans own stocks, the apparent implication being that there was a fairly broad sharing of the huge run-up in asset prices that peaked in March 2000. In fact, however, asset ownership has become even more heavily concentrated during recent years. As figure 4 shows, for example,

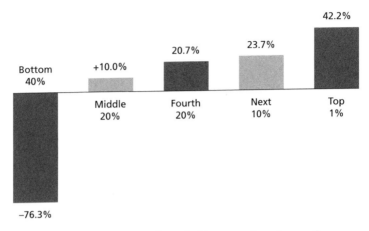

Figure 5. Changes in average household net worth, 1983–1998.
Sources: Wolff 1998; www.inequality.org.

the net worth of the median household remained virtually unchanged between 1989 and 1999, a period during which the total net worth of American households nearly doubled.

People in the middle simply don't own much stock. Because their pensions were, for the most part, defined-benefit plans rather than defined-contribution plans, they did not benefit significantly from the stock market boom of the 1990s.

As with income, the real growth in wealth came predominantly at the top. As shown in figure 5, for example, the bottom 40 percent of households actually experienced a significant decline in net worth between 1983 and 1998, a period during which the top 1 percent saw its wealth grow by more than 40 percent.

But it was within the top 1 percent that the most spectacular changes in net worth occurred. For the past several decades, *Forbes* has published a list of the estimated net worth of the four hundred richest Americans. In 1982 there were only thirteen billionaires on this list, five of them children of the Texas oil baron H. L. Hunt. By 1996 there were 179 billionaires on the Forbes list, and by 2005 there were 374. Together the Forbes four hundred are now worth more than a trillion dollars, nearly one-eighth the national income of China, a country with one billion people.

There were some 7.5 million American households with a net worth of at least a million dollars in 2004, more than 20 percent more than there had been just the year before.[1] If a net worth of a million dollars has become almost commonplace, a net worth of five million dollars still counts as real money. There were 740,000 such families in 2004, 37 percent more than there had been a year earlier.[2] Wealth at that level was once rare. Twenty-five years ago, if people worth more than five million dollars happened to find themselves in Ithaca on business, there would almost certainly have been an article about them in the *Ithaca Journal*. But now that almost three of every thousand people have a net worth that high, such events have become altogether unremarkable.

My point is not that the creation of these big fortunes is by itself a bad thing; I cite these figures merely to present a rough picture of how the distributions of income and wealth were evolving in the United States at the end of the twentieth century. In contrast to the robber barons of the nineteenth century, most of the people who have amassed today's big fortunes did so without having to crush labor unions with armies of hired thugs. And although there are obvious exceptions, most of today's wealthy did not become rich by stealing money from others who had a rightful claim to it. Rather, they invented valuable new products and services and sold them to the public.

But whatever processes may have been involved, the result has been that the distributions of income and wealth have become much more concentrated during the last several decades. Those in the middle of the income and wealth distributions have lost ground relative to those at the top, despite the absolute increases in their income and wealth. For them, to return to my first thought experiment, the United States has become much more like World A and much less like World B.

CHAPTER THREE

Inequality, Happiness, and Health

With evidence on recent trends in income and wealth inequality in hand, we are now in a position to attempt to answer the question before us: Does rising inequality harm the middle class? One way to approach it is to try to answer a closely related question: Does growing inequality make the middle class less happy? Although few economists would pose such a question, I am persuaded that much can be learned from an attempt to answer it. As a first step, we require a workable measure of happiness. So I will briefly survey some highlights from the large literature devoted to the measurement of human happiness and well-being.

Psychologists and other behavioral scientists have for several decades been trying to measure what they call *subjective well-being*.[1] I once asked Ed Diener, a pioneering researcher in this area, why he and his colleagues use that term instead of just saying *happiness*. He said, "Well, it *is* happiness that we're studying, but we'd be much less likely to get NSF grants if we called it that. They wouldn't think it was scientific enough." But even though subjective well-being and happiness have much in common, the two concepts are not identical. Subjective well-being depends in part on how one feels at a given moment, but it also entails considered judgments about the overall quality of one's life.

In practice, one of the principal measures of subjective well-being comes in the form of responses to surveys that ask people to classify themselves into one of three categories: very happy, fairly happy, or not happy. Other surveys ask subjects to respond on a ten-point scale to questions like "All things considered, how satisfied are you with your life these days?"

Economists often voice strong misgivings about such measures. What can we possibly learn, they wonder, by posing questions like that? This is the United States, after all, and most people know they are supposed to be happy here. But although some people may overstate their personal happiness levels on that account, a significant proportion are willing to admit to being only fairly happy. And a minority — a small minority, but still a sizable number — classify themselves as not happy.

What is more, people are consistent in their responses. Their answer to a given question is likely to be the same eight months from now as it is today. If we try to measure happiness in other, less direct, ways, the results accord closely with the results we get when we just ask people whether they are happy. Suppose, for example, that a subject is asked to indicate on a five-point scale the extent to which he agrees with statements like "When good things happen to me, it strongly affects me," or "I often do things for no other reason than that they might be fun." (Five points indicates "strongly agree" and one point indicates "strongly disagree.") People who strongly agree with such statements are likely to have classified themselves as happy in response to an overall

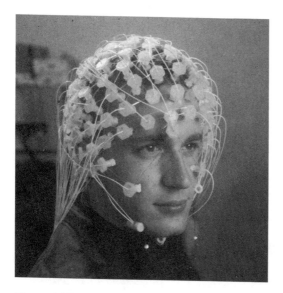

Figure 6. Electrical measurement of happiness.
Photograph courtesy of Richard J. Davidson.

happiness question. Conversely, those who strongly disagree are likely to have classified themselves as unhappy.[2]

Similarly, people who call themselves happy are much more likely to register strong agreement with statements like "When I get something I want, I feel excited and energized." Those who classify themselves as unhappy apparently do not feel that way. Happy people agree strongly that "When I am doing well at something, I love to keep at it," whereas unhappy people often seem not even to understand what such statements are getting at.

Neuroscientists also assess emotional valence by measuring asymmetries in brain waves. The device they employ, shown in figure 6, is quite remarkable. They hook you up to a host of electrodes that measure waves in electrical activity emitted from various parts of the brain. If you have brain-wave patterns emanating disproportionately from the right prefrontal region of your brain, you are much more likely to say you are not happy in response to survey questions. And you are much more likely to disagree with statements like the ones I just mentioned. In contrast, if your brain-wave patterns emanate disproportionately from the left prefrontal region, you are much more likely to call yourself happy when somebody asks you, and much more likely to agree strongly with the statements mentioned.[3]

The brain-wave data are also remarkably consistent. People whose brain waves suggest unhappiness in September are also likely to signal unhappiness in October. And those who are classified as happy in September tend to exhibit similar brain-wave patterns in October. I note in passing that the subjects in one University of Wisconsin brain-wave study happened to include a Tibetan monk who was visiting the campus for several months. In two separate measures, his brain-wave patterns were several standard deviations above the mean on the implied happiness scale.[4]

People who say they are happy or who are revealed as happy by these other methods also show other symptoms of being happy.[5] For example, they are more likely to be rated as happy by their friends. Perhaps the happiness levels of your friends are none of your business, but if you're like most people you have opinions about them. It turns out that such impressions agree closely with what people say about themselves and with how they respond to the surveys and other happiness measures.

People who are classified as happy by the various measures are more likely to initiate social contact with friends, a step that mental health professionals regard as indicative of psychological well-being. Happy persons are also more likely to respond to requests for help. My colleague Alice Isen has done an interesting experiment showing this.[6] Subjects in the treatment group found a coin she had placed in the return slot of a public telephone, a manipulation that reliably induces a temporary increase in happiness. Control subjects found the return slot empty. As they left the phone booth, subjects from both groups were approached by a stranger with a request, either for help changing a flat tire or for help picking up a spilled sack of groceries. Subjects who had found a coin — the happy subjects — were much more likely than those in the control group to assist the stranger.

People who are classified as happy by the various measures are less likely to suffer from psychosomatic illnesses, such as digestive disorders, headaches, and rapid heartbeat. Happy persons are also less likely to be absent from work and less likely to be involved in disputes at work. Happy people are less likely to seek psychological counseling. And happy people are much less likely than unhappy people to attempt suicide, the ultimate behavioral measure of unhappiness. A death initially thought to have been a suicide is immediately reinvestigated if the deceased's friends tell police that she seemed extremely happy in the days before she died.

There is, in short, a real concept here. Whether we call it happiness or subjective well-being, its measures are consistent, reliable, and valid by the usual behavioral science standards. It's a measure of something that most of us care about.

To be happy is obviously not the only objective in life. As philosophers are fond of asking, would you rather be Socrates dissatisfied or a pig satisfied? In any event, in what follows I shall assume only that becoming happier would be a good thing if it could be accomplished without giving up something else of importance.

Given that happiness can be measured reliably, we are now in a position to try to assess what links exist, if any, between inequality and happiness. We can pose questions such as "Does money buy happiness?" and "Does income inequality affect happiness in some way?"

These are old questions. In answer to the first one, Billy Graham said that "being a slave to money is a dead-end road, for money can never bring us lasting happiness and peace." Everyone recognizes the wisdom in that statement, and yet there are contrary views as well. Perhaps those who say money can't buy happiness simply don't know where to shop. What seems certain is that most of us believe that having more money would make us happier. Why would people work eighty hours a week or put up with abusive bosses if having more money didn't matter?

There are two important empirical findings on the relationship between money and happiness. Richard Easterlin first called these findings to the attention of economists in an article published in 1974, and they have held up during the years since.[7] The first is that, beyond some point, when everyone gets more money, it doesn't seem to make much difference. The light gray line in figure 7, for example, plots average happiness and the dark line plots average income in Japan between the years 1961 and 1987, a period during which income grew almost fourfold in that country. The average happiness curve during those years was flat as a pancake.

The pattern shown in figure 7, which consistently shows up in other countries as well, poses an apparent challenge for conven-

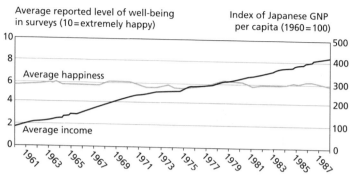

Figure 7. Average happiness versus average income over time in Japan.
Source: Veenhoven 1993.

tional economic models. If getting more income does not make people happier, why do they go to such lengths to get more income? Why, for example, do legal associates work eighty hours a week hoping to become partners in law firms? Why do tobacco company CEOs endure the public humiliation of testifying before Congress that smoking has not been shown to cause serious illnesses?

It turns out that if we measure the income-happiness relationship in a second way, income matters very much indeed. Consider figure 8, which shows this relationship for the United States during a brief period during the 1980s. When we plot average happiness versus average income for clusters of people in a given country at a given time, as in the diagram, rich people are in fact substantially happier than poor people.

The patterns portrayed in figures 7 and 8 are consistent with the view that relative income is a far better predictor of happiness than absolute income. Indeed, absolute income is not a very big determinant of variations in measured happiness in the econom-

*"Researchers say I'm not happier for being richer, but
do you know how much researchers make?"*

ically developed countries. But in extremely poor countries—
those in which people generally have too little to eat or in which
substantial numbers are cold or homeless—happiness measures
do increase when everyone's income rises. For present purposes,
however, the important point is that once absolute income
reaches a given threshold, measured happiness changes little
when everyone's income grows at the same rate. Eugene
Smolensky, for example, found that the median values of "minimum comfort" budgets reported by workers in New York City
have hovered around half the value of the national per-capita
income since the turn of the twentieth century.[8]

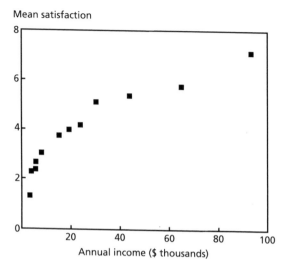

Figure 8. Income versus satisfaction in the United States, 1981–1984. Source: Diener et al. 1993.

Many psychologists seem not to understand the link between income and happiness very well, and I am puzzled by this, because my impression is that they tend to be better applied statisticians than most economists. These psychologists often claim that income doesn't matter, because when they look at the proportion of the variance in happiness explained by income in a sample of individuals observed at a moment in time, they find it to be very low—typically less than 2 percent.[9]

But that does not imply that income is an unimportant determinant of happiness. The reason that income explains such a small proportion of the variance in the happiness data is that these data are incredibly noisy. Many other factors besides your income matter a great deal for explaining how happy you are.

The most important one is the kind of temperament you inherited. But even after controlling for temperament, there is a strong positive relationship between average income and average happiness in cross-section data. If you're an unhappy person, you might be poor or you might be rich. There are many unhappy people at every income level, and also many happy ones. But if you are poor and have an unhappy temperament, you are going to be much happier than before if you get more money.

Psychologists may misapprehend the income-happiness link because they tend to work with analysis-of-variance models, which emphasize the proportion of variance attributable to various causal factors. In contrast, economists tend to work with statistical regression models, which emphasize the change in outcome that results from a given change in a causal factor. The regression approach calls our attention to the fact that even though income doesn't explain a high proportion of the variance in happiness, a given change in income is nonetheless associated with a fairly large change in happiness. And for our purposes, that's the important practical point: Significant increases in relative income give rise to significant increases in subjective well-being. And since middle-class families have fallen behind sharply in relative terms, this finding implies a corresponding reduction in well-being.

Do happiness measures vary systematically with income inequality? Andrew Oswald and David Blanchflower have done a study of American cross-section data in which they found lower happiness levels, on the average, in states with higher levels of income inequality.[10] And although it's difficult to interpret the variations we see in international happiness data, there are hints of a similar pattern there as well. The happiest people are the

Danes, and people in the other Scandinavian countries also score well above average on happiness scales. In general, income inequality declines in Europe the farther north you go. So there is at least a suggestion that lower inequality and greater happiness go together.[11]

No attempt to address the question of whether rising inequality harms the middle class can ignore the emerging literature on the links between inequality and health. Scores of careful studies have now shown that even in societies that are quite wealthy in absolute terms, greater inequality is associated with a variety of adverse health outcomes.[12]

The pioneering studies in this area, the so-called Whitehall studies, were of large samples of British civil servants. For these people, almost all of whom were well educated, earned good salaries, and had access to the excellent British National Health Service, the rates of illness and death were many times higher among low-ranking persons within each unit than among high-ranking persons, even after controlling for smoking and a variety of other behaviors known to affect health.[13]

The first Whitehall study involved 18,000 male civil servants who were between the ages of 40 and 69 in 1967–1969. Among these men, the risk of death from heart disease was less than one-third as high for men in the highest employment grade as for those in the lowest grade.[14] A second Whitehall study involved 10,000 male and female civil servants aged 35 to 55 in 1985–1988. For both sexes, the incidence of long illnesses was inversely related to job grade. Women in the lowest job grade had four times as many long illnesses as those in the highest grade.[15]

Changes in relative position have also been shown to have measurable effects on fundamental biochemical processes. In males, for example, concentrations of the sex hormone testosterone appear to fluctuate with even minor variations in local status. Reductions in status thus tend to be followed by reductions in plasma testosterone levels, whereas these levels tend to rise following increases in status.[16] A player who wins a tennis match decisively, for example, experiences a postmatch elevation in plasma testosterone, and his vanquished opponent experiences a postmatch reduction.[17] And there is some evidence from primate studies that elevated concentrations of testosterone facilitate behaviors that help achieve or maintain high status.[18]

Studies I will discuss in subsequent chapters have identified plausible candidates for the kinds of causal mechanisms that might link inequality and health. For example, longer commutes to work, which are associated with higher inequality, are known to be associated with higher morbidity and mortality. Reduced investments in public health and increased sleep deprivation, also associated with increased inequality, may contribute as well. But perhaps the most parsimonious explanation for the link between inequality and health is the one suggested by Richard Wilkinson, which is that people simply find being in a subordinate position stressful.[19] This interpretation is consistent with findings about the relationship between income inequality and the likelihood of divorce. Using U.S. Census data for 1990 and 2000, Adam Levine and I have estimated that counties with the largest increases in inequality were also the ones that experienced the largest increases in divorce rates.[20]

Research into the relationship between social rank and physiology is still in its relative infancy. And at least some respected scholars believe it is premature to be confident that causal relationships have been reliably identified.[21] Yet given the powerful

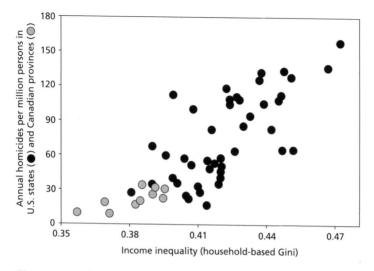

Figure 9. 1990 homicide rates in U.S. states and Canadian provinces as a function of income inequality. Source: Daly, Wilson, and Vasdev 2001.

historical relationship between social rank and survival prospects, it seems fair to say that systematic links between social rank and physiological processes that affect health would hardly be an unexpected finding.

Martin Daly, Margo Wilson, and Shawn Vasdev have shown that inequality is also linked to the risk of death by homicide.[22] Using data for both American states and Canadian provinces, they find the sharply upward-sloping relationship between homicide risk (as measured by the annual number of homicides per million persons) and income inequality (as measured by the Gini coefficient for household incomes) portrayed in figure 9. Although positive links between inequality and homicide had also been observed in previous studies based solely on U.S. data,[23] interpretation of those findings was clouded by the fact that high inequality is correlated with low average incomes in the United States. But high inequality is associated with high average incomes in Canadian data, which appears to rule out the possibility that inequality is merely a proxy for poverty in the causal relationship. As Daly, Wilson, and Vasdev conclude, "the degree to which resources are unequally distributed is a stronger determinant of levels of lethal violence in modern nation states than is the average level of material welfare."

CHAPTER FOUR

Envy or Context?

Cartoons are data. If a cartoonist produces a drawing and we laugh, that tells us something. A *New Yorker* cartoon by Robert Weber depicts a man driving by as he looks out at a man talking on an outdoor public phone during a heavy rainstorm. The motorist thinks to himself: "I was sad because I had no on-board fax until I saw a man who had no mobile phone." That what we feel we need depends on what other people have is an old idea. It is not a radical conjecture.

Yet it is an idea that does not sit comfortably. Indeed, most parents go to considerable lengths in an effort to train their children not to care too much about what others have. It's not important, we tell them; pay attention to what you have, do the best you can. This is sound advice. There will always be others with more, and to become preoccupied by that fact is a sure recipe for psychological misery. Envy is a corrosive emotion, one that we do well to discourage.

Because concerns about relative income are so often seen as a regrettable human frailty, few economists have taken them seriously in welfare analysis. It is a mistake, however, to view these concerns in such harshly pejorative terms. They are much better understood as an unavoidable consequence of the need to make the kinds of evaluative judgments we confront as we attempt to solve practical problems in our daily lives.

Think about the problems we face in a competitive environment when trying to decide what to do. We need to get feedback from the environment and then make evaluations and decisions based on those evaluations. To do this effectively, we need some basic cognitive processing power and some fast algorithms to apply in different situations. I will illustrate some of the algorithms that we seem to use with a few physical examples.

Which of the two vertical lines in figure 10 is longer? Most people respond confidently that it is the line on the right. Yet, as you can easily verify, the two lines are exactly the same length. The line on the right looks longer only because in its local frame of reference — sitting as it does between the two oblique lines — it does a bigger job of bridging the gap. In its local context, the right line is bigger. Yet in absolute terms, it has the same length as the line on the left.

If, like most people, you think that the line on the right looks longer, you have no reason to be embarrassed. It is completely normal to fall victim to this optical illusion. Indeed, if the two lines appear to be the same length to you, you might want to schedule a neurological checkup.

Local context influences not only spatial perceptions but also our evaluations of temperature. Is it a cold day today? Do you need to wear a coat? To answer questions like those, you again need an appropriate frame of reference. If it's a sixty-degree day

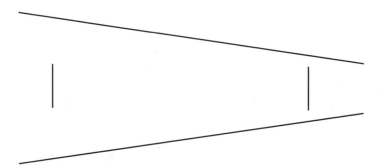

Figure 10. Which vertical line is longer?

in Miami in November, you're likely to say, "How could anyone even ask if it's cold out?" I grew up in Miami and recall vividly how cold it felt on a sixty-degree day in November as my classmates and I huddled under blankets in the stands at football games. We *knew* it was cold, and if we hadn't known to dress warmly, we'd have been miserable.

But suppose we're talking about a sixty-degree day in Montreal in February. There, too, someone who asks whether it's cold out will be seen as having asked a stupid question. Yet the answer is exactly the opposite. Of course it's *not* a cold day, as anyone could plainly see from the fact that people are in the streets in shirtsleeves celebrating the mild weather.

If your own evaluations of the weather are influenced by local context in these ways, you are completely normal. Indeed, if you were a subject in a laboratory experiment and were not influenced by your local frame of reference in these ways, neuroscientists would want to search your brain for the lesion that disrupted your evaluations. If your judgments of space and temperature are not context-sensitive, you are not a normal human being.[1]

Figure 11. 1979 Chevrolet Nova. Photograph courtesy of
Tom Thorson.

What about the role of local context when it comes to evaluations of the things we own? Suppose your car is a 1979 Chevrolet Nova (figure 11). Is it OK? It's a natural question to ask, and the answer to it will almost certainly depend on local context. If you live in Havana, Cuba, this car is not just OK, it is fabulous. To show up behind the wheel of that car would be like having a sign around your neck saying, "I am a player." It would be a clear statement about your privileged position in that society.

But if you were an aspiring film producer in Bel Air, California, the same car would not be OK. To show up there behind the wheel of that car would be like having a sign around your neck saying, "I am not a player." Successful deal makers in Bel Air earn a lot of money. Normally they drive Porsche 911s and other expensive late-model cars. They don't drive 1979 Chevy Novas.

Of course if you are *really* successful, you can show up in whatever car you please. A Charles Barsotti cartoon depicts a clown sitting in his law office behind his desk as he looks across at an obviously skeptical client. The clown says to the client, "Look at it this way: If I weren't a *very good* lawyer, could I practice in a clown costume?" So if you're Steven Spielberg or someone else who's already known to have made it big, then of course your showing up in a 1979 Chevy Nova is not a problem. It just proves that you have nothing left to prove. But unless you're Steven Spielberg, you might consider parking your Nova several blocks away. Being uneasy about being seen at the wheel of that car as an aspiring deal maker in Bel Air is not a symptom of psychological frailty.

Consider, too, the question of what constitutes adequate living space. Suppose you're the CEO of a fast-growing company in Stamford, Connecticut, and you're about to receive clients to discuss a contract. You happen to be living temporarily in a 500-square-foot apartment while contractors are completing the finishing touches on your new home outside the city. How do you feel as your clients are about to arrive? It would be completely normal for you to experience a knot of anxiety wondering how they will react when they walk in the front door. After all, few successful companies have CEOs who live in apartments that small.

But now imagine that you're the same CEO about to receive clients aboard your yacht moored at the Greenwich Marina. Your 500 square feet of onboard living space is exactly the same as the 500 square feet of living space of your current apartment. But this time you're unlikely to feel any anxiety at all about how your clients will react. The same floor space that was inadequate in the first frame of reference is much more than adequate in the second.

Is a ten-by-ten-foot bedroom big enough? If it were the master bedroom suite in your yacht at the Greenwich Marina, it would seem remarkably spacious. Yet in other contexts, a bedroom of that size might seem much too small.

Until several years ago, my wife and I occupied one of the four twelve-by-twelve-foot bedrooms on the second floor of our house, which, to one of us, seemed uncomfortably small. So we hired a contractor to merge the two twelve-by-twelve bedrooms on the opposite side of the hall. Not counting its two generous closets, our new bedroom is almost twice as large as the earlier one. We like it much better, and it doesn't seem ostentatious. Most of our friends have master bedrooms at least as large.

Whether a given bedroom seems big enough depends on local context. If we lived in Tokyo, we never would have dreamed of enlarging our twelve-by-twelve-foot bedroom. There, if we had talked to a contractor about changing our bedroom at all, it would have been to put in a partition and rent part of it out.

Another purchase decision I faced a few years ago provides a particularly vivid illustration of the importance of context. After having served me well for almost a decade, various parts of the gas grill I had bought in the late 1980s began to fail (see figure 12). First to go bad was the spark generator — the little button you push to generate the spark that fires up the gas. The grill still functioned well enough without a spark generator. You simply had to turn on the gas, wait a few seconds, and then throw a match in. (As I quickly discovered, timing was *very* important here.)

Next to fail was the sheet-metal baffle that sat atop the burners, whose purpose was to diffuse the heat across the grilling surface. Corrosion had produced a large hole in the middle of this plate, so all the heat came rushing up through that one spot. You

Figure 12. 1989 Sunbeam Grill, $89.
Photograph by author.

could work around that problem, too, by moving pieces in and out of the hot zone quickly to keep them from scorching.

After various other minor parts failed, I finally decided that it was time for a new grill. That's when I discovered that the menu of choices in this particular product category wasn't anything at all like what I'd seen when I shopped for my $89 original grill.

One offering in particular caught my eye — the Viking Front-gate Professional. I'll describe some of its features. Above the grilling surface sits an infrared bar, in front of which is an electric rotisserie that can turn two twenty-pound turkeys to perfection, while at the same time you're cooking up to forty hamburgers on the large grilling surface. Then inside there's another feature that my old Sunbeam did not have: a smoker system that — I'm quoting from the brochure here — "utilizes its own 5,000 BTU burner and watertight wood-chip drawer to season food with rich woodsy flavor." But what impressed me most were the two ancillary range-top burners that sit off to the side. Each could generate 15,000 BTUs of heat — roughly twice as much as a burner on a standard kitchen range. Why 15,000 BTUs? It turns out that if you want to do flash ethnic stir-frying, the extra heat helps to sear the flavors in. Or so I was told. The price of this grill, not including shipping and handling, was $5,000. Constructed of gleaming stainless steel with enamel accents, it was seven feet across and had ample storage underneath.

It was more grill than I wanted. When I passed on the chance to buy it, the salesman showed me a "value" model. It was smaller, lacked the rotisserie and smoker, and had only one 15,000 BTU burner. But it could deliver professional results at a value price of $1,160. What struck me at the time was that having just considered a $5,000 grill, the $1,160 model seemed like a perfectly plausible candidate to replace my Sunbeam. And although I also passed on this model in the end, it was easy to see how someone who bought it might actually think to himself what a prudent shopper he'd been. I finally bought a $250 Weber charcoal grill, one with a nice stainless steel work surface and a big dome and a chimney for lighting the charcoal. It cost almost three times as much as my old gas grill. But still, I felt frugal buying it.

Figure 13. Gisele Bundchen modeling the Victoria's
Secret Fantasy Bra, $12.5 million. Copyright 2005
J McCarthy/Wireimage.com.

Sellers are well aware of how context affects purchase decisions. For many Christmases running, for example, the Victoria's
Secret catalog highlighted one particularly expensive gift for its
readers to consider. The 1996 catalog featured Claudia Schiffer
modeling the $1 million diamond-studded Miracle Bra, the first
entry in the series. The following year, Tyra Banks arrived in an
armored car at the showroom of Harry Winston jewelers on
Fifth Avenue in New York wearing the 1997 Victoria's Secret
supergift, this time a $3 million bra ornamented with sapphires
and diamonds. The 2005 version of the bejeweled bra, modeled
by Gisele Bundchen, was listed at $12.5 million. (See figure 13.)

This pattern of escalating prices is an essential element in the public relations game. If, as the managing editor of a newspaper or fashion magazine, you've already sent a reporter to cover the $3 million garment, why send another the next year to cover it again? To attract notice, the new garment must be in some conspicuous way bigger and better, or at least more expensive. I was recently told that none of Victoria's Secret's bejeweled bras has yet been purchased by an actual customer. No matter. The jewels can easily be recycled and, more important, the mere presence of these garments in the catalog shifts the frame of reference for millions of customers, making the idea of spending only $100 on a gift undergarment seem thrifty.

Context also matters when people are confronted with questions from the happiness surveys discussed earlier. Experiments have shown, for example, that happiness levels differ substantially according to who happens to be in the room when the question is posed. Subjects rate their own happiness levels about two points higher on a ten-point scale if someone in a wheelchair is present during the survey.[2] The frame of reference that subjects employ for evaluating their own happiness levels apparently shifts in response to whatever cues happen to be salient when the question is posed.

When I was a Peace Corps volunteer in Nepal, the house I lived in had a grass roof that leaked when it rained hard. It was an extremely small house by U.S. standards; it had no plumbing and no electricity. It was a house that most families would be ashamed of in the United States. If you lived in such a house here, your children would be embarrassed to bring their friends home. Yet never once did I feel embarrassed about living in that house in Nepal, because it was actually a terrific house in that context.

Context matters in these ways for almost everybody. If you are not somebody for whom context matters, you are just not a normal person. Yet despite the obvious importance of context, modern disciples of Adam Smith have been extremely reluctant to introduce concerns about context into discussions of economic policy. Smith himself recognized these concerns as a basic component of human nature. Writing more than two centuries ago, he introduced the important idea that local consumption standards influence the goods and services that people consider essential (or "necessaries," as Smith called them). In the following passage, for example, he described the factors that influence the amount an individual must spend on clothing in order to be able to appear in public "without shame."

> By necessaries I understand not only the commodities which are indispensably necessary for the support of life, but whatever the custom of the country renders it indecent for creditable people, even of the lowest order, to be without. A linen shirt, for example, is, strictly speaking, not a necessary of life. The Greeks and Romans lived, I suppose, very comfortably though they had no linen. But in the present times, through the greater part of Europe, a creditable day-labourer would be ashamed to appear in public without a linen shirt, the want of which would be supposed to denote that disgraceful degree of poverty which, it is presumed, nobody can well fall into without extreme bad conduct. Custom, in the same manner, has rendered leather shoes a necessary of life in England. The poorest creditable person of either sex would be ashamed to appear in public without them.[3]

The absolute standard of living in the United States today is of course vastly higher than it was in Adam Smith's eighteenth-century Scotland. Yet Smith's observations apply with equal force to contemporary industrial societies. Consider, for instance, the *New York Times* correspondent Dirk Johnson's account of the experiences of Wendy Williams, a middle-school student from a low-income family in a highly prosperous community in Illinois.[4] Both of Wendy's parents are employed at low-wage jobs, and the family lives in Chateau Estates, a trailer park at which her school bus picks her up each morning.

> Watching classmates strut past in designer clothes, Wendy Williams sat silently on the yellow school bus, wearing a cheap belt and rummage-sale slacks. One boy stopped and yanked his thumb, demanding her seat.
>
> "Move it, trailer girl," he sneered.
>
> It has never been easy to live on the wrong side of the tracks. But in the economically robust 1990's, with sprawling new houses and three-car garages sprouting like cornstalks on the Midwestern prairie, the sting that comes with scarcity gets rubbed with an extra bit of salt.
>
> . . .
>
> To be without money, in so many ways, is to be left out.
>
> "I told this girl: 'That's a really awesome shirt. Where did you get it?'" said Wendy, explaining that she knew it was out of her price range, but that she wanted to join the small talk. "And she looked at me and laughed and said, 'Why would you want to know?'"
>
> A lanky, soft-spoken girl with large brown eyes, Wendy pursed her lips to hide a slight overbite that got her the nickname Rabbit, a humiliation she once begged her mother and father to avoid by sending her to an orthodontist.
>
> For struggling parents, keenly aware that adolescents agonize over the social pecking order, the styles of the moment

and the face in the mirror, there is no small sense of failure
in telling a child that she cannot have what her classmates take
for granted.

"Do you know what it's like?" asked Wendy's mother,
Veronica Williams, "to have your daughter come home and
say, 'Mom, the kids say my clothes are tacky,' and then walk
off with her head hanging low."

An adolescent in Adam Smith's eighteenth-century Scotland
would not have been much embarrassed by having a slight over-
bite, because not even the wealthiest members of society wore
braces on their teeth then. In the intervening years, however, rising living standards have altered the frame of reference that
defines an acceptable standard of cosmetic dentistry. On what
ground might we argue that inequality's toll on individuals like
Wendy Williams is unimportant because it occurs in psychological, rather than explicit monetary, terms?

Many economists appear opposed to taking such effects into
account in welfare analysis because they view them not as real
costs but merely psychological ones. I find this a very strange
position for our profession to take. Economists have always
insisted that a person's preferences are her own business. The
consumer knows best. As Jeremy Bentham famously said, a taste
for poetry is no better than a taste for pushpins, a popular parlor
game of his era. If you respect people's preferences and they
experience psychological costs from relative disadvantage, why
shouldn't those costs be taken into account in a welfare analysis?
That is something that no one has ever been able to explain
clearly to me.

The closest anyone has ever come is to say, "Well, that would just be enshrining envy for public policy purposes." This is actually a cogent concern. There are good reasons to limit envy and other corrosive emotions. But the examples just discussed don't seem to have much to do with envy. Wendy Williams, for example, doesn't really seem to envy her classmates; she just seems to feel ashamed at not being able to meet the ordinary standards of her community.

CHAPTER FIVE

The Rising Cost of Adequate

Increased spending at the top of the income distribution has imposed not only psychological costs on families in the middle, but also more tangible costs. In particular, it has raised the cost of achieving goals that most middle-class families regard as basic.

Consider, for example, the price a middle-class family must pay in order to secure housing that is adequate by community standards. Increased expenditures on housing by top earners appear to have launched an "expenditure cascade" that has resulted in increased housing expenditures even among those whose incomes have not risen. The process starts when sharply higher incomes prompt top earners to build larger mansions. To the extent that middle-income families even notice these mansions, there is no evidence that they are offended by them. On the contrary, many seem to derive pleasure from seeing images of them in magazines and on television.

But for those just below the top, the new mansions alter the frame of reference that defines what kind of house is considered necessary or desirable. Perhaps it is now the custom to host one's daughter's wedding reception in the home, or to host larger dinner parties. And when the near rich, in turn, build larger houses, others just below them find their own 10,000-square-foot houses no longer adequate, and so on all the way down the income ladder. Thus the median size of a newly constructed house in the United States, which stood at 1,600 square feet in 1980, had risen to more than 2,100 square feet by 2001, despite the fact that the median family's real income had changed little in the intervening years (see figure 3).[1]

The escalating price of the median house creates a problem for middle-income families, because the quality of public schools in the United States is closely linked to local property taxes, which in turn depend on local real estate prices. In the light of evidence that any given student's achievement level rises with the average socioeconomic status of his or her classmates, property values and school quality will be positively linked even in jurisdictions in which school budgets are largely independent of local property values.

Now, we may safely assume that most middle-class families aspire to send their children to schools of at least average quality. Indeed, parents who felt completely at ease with the prospect of their children attending below-average schools would be judged harshly in most communities. The difficulty is that middle-income families cannot send their children to schools of average quality now without spending significantly more, in real terms, than in 1980.

Middle-income families thus confront a painful dilemma.

They can either send their children to a school of average quality by purchasing a house that is larger and more expensive than they can comfortably afford, or they can buy a smaller house that is within their budget and send their children to a below-average school. To see why so many families might find the former option more compelling, we need not assume that they are strongly prone to envy or jealousy.

The price of the median house has escalated not just because houses have gotten bigger, but also because of the higher premium that desirable locations now command. Because the Wildavsky Forum takes place in Berkeley, in preparing the lecture on which this book is based I did a little digging to see how house prices had been changing in the Bay Area. Table 1 shows four representative middle-class houses. I will focus on the one in North Oakland because of its proximity to the Berkeley campus. It's a house with 1,715 square feet built in 1911, and it sold in 1970 for $23,500. In 1998 the same house sold for $290,000. In 1970 the average income for the North Oakland community was $11,279. By 1998, it was $50,840. Average income thus increased by a factor of only five during the same span that the price of this house grew by a factor of twelve. In table 1 we see essentially the same pattern for the other Bay Area communities listed.

I do not claim that the price trajectories shown in table 1 are the result solely of rising income inequality. Many other factors are in play, such as the rapid population growth of the Bay Area during this period. But Bjornulf Ostvik-White has identified a systematic positive relationship between median house prices and income inequality at the school district level in 2000 Census data.[2]

Table 1. A history of four Bay Area houses

Location	Sunnyvale	San Rafael	San Carlos	N. Oakland
Number of bedrooms				
	3	3	2	4
Number of baths				
	2	2	1	2
Size in square feet				
	1,686	1,552	1,082	1,715
Year built	1962	1958	1933	1911
Price				
1970	$35,000	$34,500	$28,500	$23,500
1998	$525,000	$355,000	$420,000	$290,000
Average income				
1970	$13,583	$16,046	$16,233	$11,279
1998	$72,480	$74,920	$92,680	$50,840
Since 1970				
Income increase				
	5X	5X	6X	5X
Housing price increase				
	15X	10X	15X	12X

Source: Curiel, Minton, and McLeod 1999.

Middle-class families also face additional pressure to spend more on cars, for in this domain as well, we see evidence of an expenditure cascade. Higher incomes at the top have induced top earners to buy cars that are faster, more luxuriously appointed, and heavier than those purchased by their counterparts two decades earlier. But the same changes have occurred even for automobiles marketed directly to middle-income consumers, whose incomes have risen little. Today's entry-level Honda Civic, for example, at 2,500 pounds is about the same size as 1985's Honda Accord, whose current model weighs 3,200 pounds. For about the same real price, an Accord buyer in 1985 could buy today's Civic and in the process do better on virtually every absolute performance dimension. The new Civic is faster and more reliable than the old Accord. It has nicer upholstery and a better sound system. And it even gets better gas mileage.

But people who buy a 2,500-pound Civic today will incur a significant risk that they wouldn't have incurred in their 1985 Accords, because they must now share the road with 6,000-pound Lincoln Navigators and 7,500-pound Ford Excursions. The odds of being killed in a collision rise roughly fivefold if your car is struck by one of these large vehicles.[3] To explain why many families might decide against today's Honda Civic, we need not assume that they are driven by envy or other psychological frailties.

Consider, too, how increased spending on clothing by top earners has affected the amount a middle-class job seeker must spend on a professional wardrobe. First impressions count for a lot during job interviews, and as apparel manufacturers are fond of reminding us, we never get a second chance to make a first impression. Of course, if one job candidate is clearly much better qualified than others, the clothing he or she wears during job interviews is unlikely to make much difference. But competition is stiff for jobs that pay well and offer opportunities for advancement. Typically there are many well-qualified candidates for each desirable job, so candidates are prudent to take whatever steps they can to gain an edge.

The problem is that looking good is an inherently relative concept. A nice suit is one that compares favorably with those worn by others in the same local environment. If others begin wearing suits of higher quality, you become less likely to make a favorable impression on interviewers. Your best response might be to spend more on clothing as well, to preserve your chances of landing the job you want.

From the collective vantage point, there is an obvious inefficiency here, since when everyone spends more on clothing, each candidate's probability of success remains the same as before. But from the perspective of the individual buyer, such expenditures are anything but inefficient. To the extent that wearing the right suit, driving the right car, wearing the right watch, or living in the right neighborhood may help someone land the right job or a big contract, these expenditures are more like investments than true consumption. But from the collective vantage point, they are extremely inefficient investments, for when all spend more, their return falls to zero.

Even the gifts that middle-income families feel compelled to give have been affected by the greater affluence of top earners. Suppose you have been invited to a professional associate's home for dinner and want to bring a bottle of wine for your host. What should you bring? John Brecher and Dorothy Gaiter, whose unpretentious, value-oriented wine column appears each Friday in the *Wall Street Journal*'s weekend section, devoted a column to precisely this question. "Ask a respected wine merchant to suggest an unusual wine, one that your host is unlikely to have tried before," they sensibly recommended. "And plan on spending about $30."[4]

"We didn't have time to pick up a bottle of wine, but this is what we would have spent."

Why should you spend so much, given that many wines available today for less than $10 are far better than the wines drunk by kings of France in centuries past? In part because you have an interest not only in how the wine tastes, but also in how your gift will be interpreted. Giving an inexpensive wine might be read as a statement that the relationship is unimportant. So unless you really *don't* care about the relationship, the extra $20 is probably worth spending. Extra spending caused by growing wealth and income at the top puts additional pressure on gift givers up and down the income ladder. When others spend more for gifts at weddings, anniversaries, birthdays, and other special occasions, the rest of us must follow suit or else risk being seen as people who just don't care.

I have suggested that rising inequality entails not only psychological costs, but more tangible costs as well. When I posed the thought experiment involving the choice between a relatively big, but absolutely small, house in World B and a relatively small, but absolutely big, house in World A, I imagined that most of you would focus on the psychological consequences of living in a relatively small house.

But perhaps many of you thought also of the more concrete consequences of having low economic rank when you thought about that choice — in particular, that if you chose World A, your neighborhood might be unsafe or you wouldn't be able to send your children to a good school. I myself think about the thought experiment in those terms, but I realize that's no indication of how others might think about it.

In any case, it's often hard to separate psychological consequences of low rank from other forms of consequences. We know, for example, that where you stand in the consumption distribution affects who will find you interesting as a potential marriage partner. At a recent conference I had a conversation with a law professor from San Francisco who had moved from full-time to half-time faculty status several years earlier. He had a cabin in the Sierras and wanted to spend more time there. He had been divorced and wanted to remarry. But although he met numerous women he found attractive at social events, he described how they would invariably lose interest in further conversation with him the moment he revealed that he was teaching only half-time. For him, the switch to half-time status seemed to function like a

"I know you young guys have a hard time believing it, but there was a time—and not all that long ago—when a man telling a woman he was in investment banking could expect a yawn."

tattoo on his forehead saying that he was no longer important, no longer an interesting person. Was that a psychological consequence of his status or a real one? In the end, it is perhaps a distinction without a difference.

CHAPTER SIX

Why Do We Care about Rank?

Being concerned with how your house compares with other people's houses makes sense for purely practical reasons, because the relative price of your house influences, among other things, how safe your neighborhood will be and the kind of schools your children will attend. It is possible that many people care about relative house size only for these practical reasons, not because of any inherent concern about relative size per se. In that case, people would generally try to keep up with community consumption standards whenever doing so promised to influence real outcomes they cared about, but would otherwise tend to ignore the spending of others.

It is also possible, however, that relative resource holdings influence real outcomes with sufficient frequency that the simplest evolutionary solution available was to craft a human nervous system that cared about relative position directly. There is a large literature that lends support to the second possibility. I have

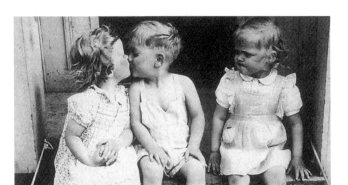

Figure 14. *Il Bacio* (The Kiss of Death). Photograph courtesy of Furman S. Baldwin. Copyright 2007 Tushita Verlag GmbH, Duisburg, Germany.

discussed this literature in detail elsewhere, so I will offer just a brief summary here of the general issues involved.[1]

The possibility that positional concerns are innate will strike few parents as wildly implausible. Notice the pained expression on the face of the toddler on the right in figure 14. Without more information to go on, it is impossible to know for sure why she is upset. But a plausible conjecture is that her mood would have been brighter had the boy sitting next to her not been present, because then she would not have been so forcefully reminded of a pleasurable experience that she was not experiencing at that moment.

Are such reactions an inborn feature of human nature? Many

insist not. Those who endorse the tabula rasa view of human nature, for example, believe that they are largely the product of social and cultural conditioning. But although cultural forces surely do explain much of our behavior, I find it difficult to believe that the girl in the photograph could have suppressed her reaction entirely, even if she had been exposed to a lifetime of careful conditioning with that specific aim in mind.

I came to this view in part because of an experiment I did years ago with my two oldest sons when they were five and seven years of age. This experiment took three days. On day one, I poured each of them a full glass of orange juice. On day two, I poured each only half a glass. Then, on day three, I poured David (then age seven) seven-eighths of a glass and Jason (then age five) only three-quarters of a glass. (See figure 15.) (I am not sure that a human subjects committee would approve this experiment today.)

You can guess what happened. On the first two days, each drank his juice without comment. In particular, neither asked on day two why he'd gotten only half as much as the day before. But things played out differently on day three. Jason looked first at his own glass, then over at his brother's, then back at his own, his face registering growing signs of distress. It was obvious that he was struggling not to react. But finally he blurted out, "That's not fair; he *always* gets more than me!"

It was hardly the first time, of course, that one of them had reacted in this way to a perceived inequity. But as on all other similar occasions, I seized the opportunity to give my little speech about the futility of worrying about such things. "Just pay attention to your own business, it doesn't matter what he has. If you drink your juice and are still thirsty, I'll give you some more." Most parents I know say things of this sort to their children when

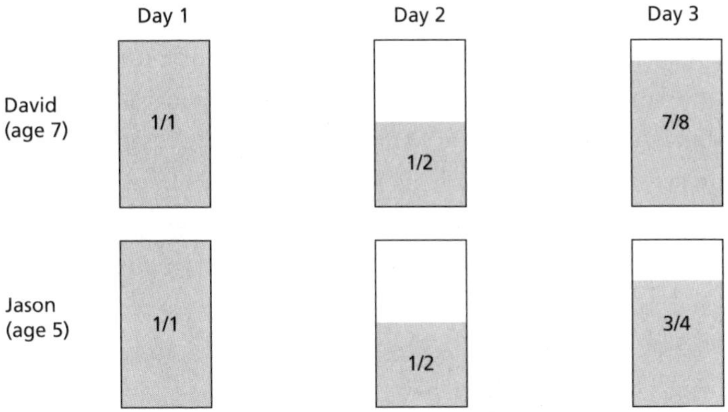

Figure 15. The orange juice experiment.

they complain about similar minor inequities. This experiment persuaded me that if cultural conditioning had anything at all to do with my son's reaction, it had made it weaker than it otherwise would have been.

Efforts to suppress such reactions eventually bear fruit. Indeed, those individuals who reach adulthood without having learned to keep their mouths shut in these situations quickly earn reputations as social boors. But the underlying reactions themselves are never completely extinguished.

I once attended an interdisciplinary conference that had been organized by a committee of humanities professors. Another economist and I were on the program together, and we were given a total of ninety minutes to present our two papers. In the immediately preceding session, two English professors had been given a total of two hours for their papers. My economist colleague and I both noticed the difference. We realized that it would have been ungracious to complain, and we didn't. But we noticed.

Would we really want our children to go out in the world not noticing things like that? Would we want them not to feel bad when their performances didn't meet local standards? Suppose your daughter were about to marry a man whose reaction to getting an F on a math test was "Who cares?" Even if his performance on that exam was one that would have earned him an A at some less demanding institution, most parents would feel uncomfortable if he simply didn't care at all.

If we adopt the biologist's view that human motivation was shaped by natural selection, it is no surprise that people might be highly aversive to positions of low rank. In the Darwinian view, animal drives were selected for their capacity to motivate behaviors that contribute to reproductive success. Reproductive success, in turn, is fundamentally about resource acquisition: other things being equal, the more resources an animal has, the more progeny it leaves behind. What matters is not the absolute number of offspring an individual has, but rather how its progeny compare in number with those of other individuals. A specific trait will thus be favored by natural selection less because it facilitates resource acquisition in absolute terms than because it confers an advantage in relative terms.

Frequent famines were an important challenge in early human societies. But even in the most severe famines, there was always some food. Those with relatively high resource holdings got fed, while others often starved. On the plausible assumption that individuals with the strongest concerns about relative resource holdings were most inclined to expend the effort necessary to achieve high rank, such individuals would have been more likely than others to survive food shortages.

Relative resource holdings were also important in implicit

markets for marriage partners. In most early human societies, high-ranking males took multiple wives, leaving many low-ranking males with none. Even in contemporary societies, sexual attractiveness is strongly linked to relative resource holdings. So here, too, theory predicts that natural selection will favor individuals with the strongest concerns about relative resource holdings.

Evolutionary theory also helps identify the specific reference groups that are likely to matter most. In evolutionary terms, falling behind one's local rivals can be lethal, whereas comparisons with others who are distant in time or space are typically irrelevant. And as the empirical studies I will discuss in a moment confirm, it is local rank that matters most.

One problem confronting all studies that attempt to assess the importance of relative income is that we never know whose incomes people care about. Those of coworkers who occupy adjacent offices? Those of neighbors? Those of classmates from high school or college? Identifying the relevant reference group has always proved a formidable challenge.

A study by David Neumark and Andrew Postlewaite offers a creative response to this challenge. Neumark and Postlewaite examined the labor market behavior of a large sample of biological full sisters.[2] They constructed their sample so that in each pair of sisters, at least one did not work in paid employment outside the home. Their goal was to investigate the factors that influenced whether the other sister in each pair would seek work outside the home. Their statistical regression model contained the usual economic suspects — the unemployment rate in the local labor market, the wage rate, and the amount of human capital individuals had. They also included a variable indicating whether the husband of the sister who was not employed earned more than the husband of the other sister.

None of the usual economic variables had much influence on the second sister's choice of whether to seek paid employment. In fact, the only important variable in their study turned out to be the husbands' relative incomes. A woman whose sister's husband earned more than her own husband was 16 to 25 percent more likely to seek paid employment than one whose own husband earned more than her sister's husband. This study thus confirms what H. L. Mencken knew intuitively when he defined a wealthy man as one who earns a hundred dollars a year more than his wife's sister's husband.

The hypothesis that local rank matters most also has testable implications for the distribution of wages within firms.[3] Suppose we define a worker's local rank in the workplace as his rank vis-à-vis coworkers in their firm's pay distribution. Standard economic theory says that workers will be paid the value of what they produce for their employers. But if workers care about local rank and cannot be forced to remain with a firm against their wishes, then there can be no stable equilibrium in which workers of unequal productivity in a firm are paid the respective values of what they contribute. After all, workers near the bottom of the pay distribution in such a firm could leave and join a new firm consisting only of workers whose productivities were equal to their own, thereby escaping the burden of low rank. If firms paid each worker exactly the value of her productive contribution, the only stable outcome would thus be for each firm to consist of workers with the same level of productivity.

Local rank is a reciprocal phenomenon. High-ranked positions, and the satisfaction that derives from them, cannot exist unless they occur in tandem with positions of low rank. So although low-ranked workers gain when they leave a firm that pays them only their marginal products, their absence imposes a cost on the formerly high-ranked workers in the abandoned firm.

If high local rank is a normal good — that is, if the amount people are willing to pay for it rises with income — then the gain to the low-ranked workers who leave will be smaller than the corresponding loss to their high-ranked colleagues who remain. Both groups can thus be made better off if the high-ranked workers compensate the low-ranked workers to remain. This is, in effect, what happens when the distribution of pay is compressed relative to the corresponding distribution of productivity. Under such a pay schedule, the high-ranked members of any firm may be said to purchase their high local rank from their less productive coworkers.

Considering the labor market as a whole, those who care least about local rank will do best to join firms in which most workers are more productive than themselves. As lesser-ranked members in these firms, they will receive extra compensation. People who care most strongly about rank, by contrast, will choose firms in which most other workers are less productive than themselves. For the privilege of occupying top-ranked positions in those firms, they will have to work for less than the value of what they produce. For any given job category within each firm, the equilibrium distribution of wages will be more compressed than the corresponding distribution of marginal products. For example, among accountants working for General Motors, the most productive individuals will be paid less than in proportion to the value of what they contribute, while the least productive individuals will be paid more. In effect, the labor market serves up com-

"O.K., *if you can't see your way to giving me a pay raise, how about giving Parkerson a pay cut?*"

pensating wage differentials for local rank, much as it does for other nonpecuniary employment conditions. Such wage compression, which is widely observed, is inconsistent with models in which local rank has no value.

In sum, although it is true that having high local rank confers tangible benefits in many specific circumstances, available evidence suggests that people care about relative position even when tangible rewards do not depend on local rank. High relative position appears to be of intrinsic value.

CHAPTER SEVEN

What Types of Consumption Are Most Sensitive to Context?

The Darwinian perspective on human motivation suggests that concerns about rank should vary in accordance with the extent to which relative consumption in different categories contributes to reproductive success. In this chapter I will consider examples of the kinds of hypotheses suggested by the Darwinian perspective and discuss how available evidence bears on each of them.

LEISURE

Consider the trade-off faced by each individual between increased consumption of leisure, on the one hand, and increased acquisition of material resources, on the other. When threats to survival are acute, as during famines, those who stand high in the distribution of material resources are more likely to get enough to eat. In contrast, those who emphasize leisure over material resource acquisition often starve. So even though everyone might enjoy greater health and well-being if all consumed more leisure, it may not be advantageous for individuals to consume more leisure unilaterally.

Sara Solnick and David Hemenway have conducted several surveys in which they ask participants to choose between hypothetical worlds in the manner illustrated in the two thought experiments discussed in chapter 1.[1] Response patterns in these surveys consistently reveal leisure to be highly valued by most individuals, regardless of context. In the same spirit, Renee Landers, James Rebitzer, and Lowell Taylor asked associates in large law firms which they would prefer: their current situation, or an otherwise similar one with an across-the-board cut of 10 percent in both hours and pay.[2] By an overwhelming margin, respondents chose the latter. Similar results have been found in other countries. For example, Swedish survey respondents considered income more positional (that is, more dependent for its value on comparison within the local context) than leisure.[3]

Changes in the distribution of income provide yet another opportunity to test whether leisure is a nonpositional good. One of the core findings of behavioral economics is loss aversion, the tendency for the pain caused by a loss of given magnitude to be greater than the pleasure caused by a gain of the same size. When income inequality increases, the expectation is thus that the pain experienced by those who fall behind is greater than the pleasure experienced by those who pull ahead. If leisure is less positional on average than other categories of consumption, it then follows that a rise in income inequality will cause a net increase in hours worked, as those who have fallen behind attempt to undo the injury they have experienced. Samuel Bowles and Yongjin Park found that total hours worked, both across countries and over time within countries, are in fact positively associated with higher earnings inequality.[4] Models that incorporate positional concerns predict these links.[5] Traditional labor market models do not.

As discussed in chapter 1, if positional concerns differ across categories, expenditure arms races focused on positional goods will produce a welfare-reducing diversion of resources from nonpositional goods. So if leisure is less positional than other categories of consumption on average, the tendency will be for people to consume too little leisure and spend too much on other categories of consumption.

Regulations, like cartoons, are data. The categories of behavior society chooses to regulate reflect social judgments about the relevant deficits and excesses. In the case of leisure, almost all countries encourage leisure consumption through regulation and social norms. Long before governments became involved, religions attempted to encourage leisure consumption by designating Sabbath days on which work was forbidden. In the United States, the Fair Labor Standards Act encourages shorter working hours by its provision requiring premium pay for labor performed in excess of eight hours per day, forty hours per week, or on national holidays. European regulations are even stricter in their support of shorter hours. And many jurisdictions continue to enforce blue laws, which make it unlawful for establishments to remain open during certain periods.

If so many countries actively intervene to constrain the number of hours that people would otherwise choose to work in unregulated markets, it must be because people believe that working longer hours would reduce welfare. The conventional explanations offered for these regulations are far from compelling. Thus, although France defended its recent requirement of a thirty-five-hour workweek on the grounds that it was needed to stimulate job creation, such stimulus effects have never been demonstrated. Similarly, although many have defended hours regulations as needed to protect workers from employers with market power, the constraints imposed by such regulations typically apply primarily to hourly workers in low-wage labor markets, which are among the most highly competitive by conventional yardsticks. Salaried workers in high-wage labor markets are relatively unconstrained by hours regulations, even though their employers are much more likely to occupy dominant market positions. If exploitation were the problem, it would be these workers who most needed protection. The observed patterns of regulation are consistent with the hypothesis that leisure gets short shrift because of positional concerns.

ENVIRONMENTAL AMENITIES

The same considerations that suggest that leisure should rank low on the positionality scale suggest a similarly low ranking for other nonmaterial consumption amenities, such as freedom from noise and pollution. By the same token, workplace amenities such as grievance procedures, additional variety, and comfort features should weigh less heavily in positional competition than the wage income that must be sacrificed to obtain them.

Labor legislation in countries around the globe regulates not just hours but also a variety of other aspects of the labor contract. In many places, the law mandates specific workplace grievance procedures, and some countries have adopted statutes that attempt to make the workplace more democratic. These regulations are also consistent with the hypothesis that such amenities would otherwise be underprovided because of positional concerns.

INVESTMENT IN CHILDREN

To have raised offspring that are well equipped to compete in their cohort is one of the most conspicuous yardsticks by which success is measured in the Darwinian framework. This task is fruitfully viewed as a contest. Most parents, for example, want their children to hold interesting, well-paying jobs some day, but such adjectives are inherently context-dependent. Thus a well-paying job is simply one that pays better than most other jobs. As in virtually every contest, contestants attempting to launch their children well in life take a variety of steps to keep pace with or surpass their rivals. Accordingly, categories of expenditure that contribute to this goal, such as expenditures on schooling, should be highly positional.

One particularly sensitive step in the contest to launch one's children successfully is the decision about when a child should begin school. Looking ahead, parents know that applicants are admitted to the most selective universities on the basis of having performed well relative to their classmates. Having one's child start kindergarten a year later than others would thus confer an advantage, because it would make the child bigger, stronger, and more intelligent relative to his classmates. But because other parents could easily respond by holding their own children back, the unregulated equilibrium might well be one in which most children would not start kindergarten until eight or nine years of age. Socially, that outcome is clearly inefficient, and most jurisdictions have enacted laws making school attendance by six-year-olds mandatory. Viewed as data, these regulations are consistent with the hypothesis that investments in children are highly positional.

In the United States, one of the most important investments a family can make in its children's future is to buy a house in a good school district. As discussed in chapter 5, the quality of a neighborhood school is strongly correlated with the average price of houses in the neighborhood. This is true in part because local property taxes are a major source of school funding. But because of the importance of peer effects in the classroom, the better schools tend to be located in more expensive neighborhoods even in countries in which school budgets are independent of local property taxes. Yet no matter how much every family spends on housing, the inescapable mathematical logic of musical chairs assures that half of all children will attend schools in the bottom half of the school quality distribution.

There is considerable evidence for the existence of bidding wars for houses in the best school districts. As Elizabeth Warren and Amelia Tyagi have shown, for example, most of the extra income earned by families as a result of the move to two-earner couples was consumed by higher housing prices as these families sought to buy homes in safer neighborhoods with better schools.[6] Warren and Tyagi also present evidence that each time the credit industry relaxed its terms by permitting lower down payments and longer payoff periods for home mortgages, the primary effect was again a bidding war for these same preferred neighborhoods.

If regulations can be viewed as data that shed light on the nature of positional concerns, the same may be true of the ways in which we choose to finance educational services. The hypothesis that investment in education of children is highly positional predicts that we should find it attractive to adopt mechanisms for paying for education that discourage expenditure arms races. The principal education finance schemes employed in the United States include just such a design feature.

Most jurisdictions levy taxes that entitle children to "free" public education. Parents also have the option of purchasing private education, but those who do so must continue to pay their school taxes. To improve upon the option of sending one's child to the public schools, a family must essentially forfeit its entitlement to free educational services and start purchasing educational services from scratch in the private sector. This arrangement creates a sharp disincentive to spending more than the per-pupil allotment specified in the public school budget.[7]

We could have chosen different arrangements. Under a voucher system of educational finance, for example, a family could boost the amount of educational services it purchased for its children without forfeiting the amount it had paid in school taxes. Under such a system, many families would undoubtedly find it attractive to give their children a little more than called for in the basic public plan. But again, the concept of a "good education" is context-dependent. As families responded to the incentive to spend more, a side effect would be to devalue the education received by others, thus imposing pressure on them to increase their spending as well.

Except for the possible fact that it might encourage an expenditure arms race, a voucher scheme appears attractive in numerous other respects. For example, voucher proponents have argued that the system would stimulate quality improvements and cost reductions of the sort generally associated with increased competition in other sectors. Distributional objections to vouchers could easily be addressed by making the vouchers progressive. That we have nonetheless rejected the voucher approach is consistent with the hypothesis that our current method of educational finance, for all its flaws, has the important virtue of keeping educational expenditures under control.

VISIBILITY

By their very nature, concerns about position cannot focus on a given category unless relative consumption in that category can be measured. Other things being equal, categories of consumption that are not readily observed should thus be relatively less positional. But observability is a necessary, not sufficient, condition for positionality. The fact that others can readily observe whether someone is a smoker, for example, does not make smoking a positional good.

In a 2004 paper, Ori Heffetz attempted to test the hypothesis that the observability of an expenditure category predicts the extent to which valuations in that category are positional.[8] On the basis of a detailed telephone survey, Heffetz assigned a visibility index, or "vindex," to more than thirty categories of expenditure recorded by the Consumer Expenditure Survey. Categories with the highest vindex values included cars, jewelry, and clothing; those with the lowest visibility included car insurance, life insurance, and household utilities. Heffetz found that the more visible a good is, the more likely it is to be positional.

SAFETY AND INSURANCE

Many expenditures, such as those on accident prevention and insurance, yield benefits only in states of the world that occur with very low probability. As Arthur Robson and others have argued, the Darwinian perspective on human motivation suggests a risk-seeking posture toward such expenditures, particularly for males.[9] As noted earlier, most human societies have been polygynous, and in such societies the highest-ranking males typically sire a disproportionate share of all offspring. This skewed payoff structure encourages high-variance strategies. The analogy is often cited to a football team that finds itself substantially behind in the fourth quarter. If it sticks to a low-variance running strategy, it is almost sure to lose. But if it switches to a high-variance passing game, it creates at least a slim chance of winning. By the same logic, many males in polygynous societies may stand little chance of marrying unless they adopt similarly risky strategies.

From a collective perspective, however, the payoff to male risk-taking is smaller than it appears to each individual male. The Darwinian prediction, then, is that the income that results from a successful risk is more positional than the safety one would enjoy by abstaining from taking risks. The fact that expenditures on safety and insurance are also relatively difficult for others to observe reinforces the prediction that these categories will be nonpositional.

In surveys involving students at Cornell University, I have substituted the following thought experiment for the second thought experiment discussed in chapter 1: "Your choice is between World C, in which you would have a 2 in 100,000 chance of being killed on the job each year, and others would have a 1 in 100,000 chance of being killed; and World D, in which you would have a 4 in 100,000 chance of being killed on the job each year, while others would have an 8 in 100,000 chance of being killed." Here again, the overwhelming majority pick C, indicating a preference for greater absolute safety at the expense of lower relative safety. Similar results have been found elsewhere. Thus, in a Swedish survey, respondents considered the monetary value of a company car more positional than its safety.[10]

The hypothesis that expenditures on safety and insurance rank low on the positionality scale implies a tendency for unregulated individual expenditures in these categories to fall short of their respective socially optimal values. And most societies have enacted various forms of legislation the effect of which is to increase expenditures in these categories.

Some will be skeptical that many labor contract regulations are attempts to stimulate consumption of nonpositional goods such as workplace safety. After all, the drafters of the legislation creating those regulations said nothing about positional concerns. They believed that they were protecting workers from exploitation by firms with market power, or that they were protecting workers from the consequences of their own ignorance or shortsightedness with respect to safety risks.

But while those rationales for regulation might have been plausible in specific instances, in the most important arenas they make little sense. For one thing, the metaphor of the company town (in which workers have no alternative to their current employer) is largely outdated. The labor markets in which safety regulations bind most tightly are typically the very ones in which employers compete most vigorously with one another in the hiring process. And while there are undoubtedly some risks to health and safety that are poorly understood by workers, in many other cases, workers seem well aware of the specific risks they face. Coal miners, for example, are certainly aware that a lifetime in the mines means a substantial risk of contracting black lung disease.

The positional account, by contrast, stresses that even in perfectly informed, competitive labor markets, risks that rational workers find collectively unattractive will often be attractive to them individually. A worker will accept a riskier job at higher pay because doing so will help her buy something important she wants, such as a house in a safer neighborhood with better schools.

In taking this step, she need not be aware — indeed, in most cases, she will not be aware at all — of feeling envious of her neighbors. Someone living in a marginal neighborhood is not worried that her neighbors are sending their children to a better school than her own children attend. Their children all go to the very same school. Their shared concern is that they cannot afford to send their children to a better one. If their interests are in conflict, it is unlikely that they are aware of it. Here again, behaviors driven by positional concerns often have little or nothing to do with envy.

SIGNALS OF ABILITY

Within specific labor markets, income and ability tend to be strongly correlated. And because observable consumption and income are also strongly correlated, observable consumption will often be a crude but effective predictor of ability. To the extent that it is individually advantageous to be seen by others as someone with high ability, the tendency will be to steer expenditures in favor of consumption categories that signal high ability. The prediction is that expenditures in these categories will run higher in environments in which independent measures of ability are less readily available.

In some occupations, the correlation between income and the underlying abilities that are valued most highly is much larger than in others. Among trial lawyers, for example, the link between income and ability is much stronger than it is in the case of university professors within any given discipline. Expenditures on items such as cars, clothing, and jewelry should thus serve as more effective signals of ability for lawyers than for professors. This observation suggests that lawyers with a given income will spend more on cars and clothing than will professors with that same income. A related prediction is that the difference between the two groups will be greater in large cities than in small cities, since other sources of information about ability are likely to be more easily accessible in small cities. These predictions fit casual impressions, but I know of no specific study that has attempted to test them systematically.

SAVINGS

Savings might also be predicted to be nonpositional on grounds of unobservability. Yet if reduced savings today means reduced capacity to spend on positional consumption in the future, the mere fact that current savings is unobservable is not decisive. Recent work in behavioral economics has identified a general tendency to discount future costs and benefits much more heavily than assumed in traditional economic models. Perhaps the problem is that whereas the current consequences of savings decisions can be experienced directly, their future consequences must be imagined. If so, then we would expect savings to be nonpositional.

Alternatively, it may be that expenditures early in life are inherently more positional than those occurring later. Suppose, for example, that a parent must choose between putting money aside to support a comfortable standard of living during retirement or using that same money toward a down payment on a house in a better school district. As noted earlier, expenditures on school quality are predicted to be highly positional. And since these expenditures occur early in life, the prediction is that their positional nature will tend to crowd out savings.

In his 1949 book *Income, Saving, and the Theory of Consumer Behavior*, James Duesenberry argued that saving is positional and presented evidence to that effect. The subsequent history of economists' attempts to explain saving behavior is a powerful case study in the sociology of knowledge. In brief, these attempts can be characterized as attempts to offer nonpositional, or context-free, explanations for the same patterns in the data. Since this history speaks directly to the important issue I raised in the preface, it merits a close look.

Any successful consumption theory must accommodate three basic patterns: the rich save at higher rates than the poor; national savings rates remain roughly constant as income grows; and national consumption is more stable than national income over short periods.

The first two patterns appear contradictory: If the rich save at higher rates, savings rates should rise over time as everyone becomes richer. Yet this does not happen. Duesenberry suggested that the explanation of the discrepancy is that poverty is relative. The poor save at lower rates, he argued, because the higher spending of others kindles aspirations they find difficult to meet. This difficulty persists no matter how much national income grows; hence the failure of national savings rates to rise over time.

To explain the short-run rigidity of consumption, Duesenberry argued that families look not only to the living standards of others, but also to their own past experience. The high standard enjoyed by a formerly prosperous family thus constitutes a frame of reference that makes cutbacks difficult, which helps explain why consumption levels change little during recessions.

Despite Duesenberry's apparent success, many economists felt uncomfortable with his relative-income hypothesis, which to them seemed more like sociology or psychology than economics. The profession was therefore immediately receptive to alternative theories that sidestepped those disciplines. Foremost among them was Milton Friedman's permanent-income hypothesis, which still dominates research on spending.[11]

Friedman argued that a family's current spending depends not on its current income, but rather on its long-run average, or permanent, income. Because economic theory predicts that people prefer steady consumption paths to highly variable ones, Friedman argued that people would smooth their spending — saving windfall income gains and drawing down savings to cover windfall losses. Consumption should thus be more stable than income over short periods. Friedman also argued that a family's savings rate should be independent of its income, leading him to predict the long-run stability of national savings rates.

Friedman dismissed the high savings rates of the rich as a statistical artifact. Because many of those with high measured incomes in any given year will have enjoyed positive windfalls, their permanent incomes will be lower, on average, than their measured incomes for that year. So if they save windfall gains, they will save a higher proportion of their measured incomes than of their permanent incomes. The converse holds for those with low measured incomes in any given year, who will have experienced a preponderance of windfall losses that year.

Although this is a tidy story, its fundamental premises are contradicted by the data. As numerous careful studies have shown, for example, savings rates rise sharply with permanent income. Friedman's defenders responded by arguing that rich consumers want to bequeath money to their children. But why should the poor lack this motive? Another problem is that people consume windfall income at almost the same rate as permanent income.[12] To this, Friedman responded that consumers appear to have unexpectedly short planning horizons. But if so, then consumption does not really depend primarily on permanent income.

Strangest of all, Friedman's theory assumes that context has absolutely no effect on judgments about living standards. It predicts, for example, that an investment banker will remain equally satisfied with his twin-engine Cessna even after discovering that his new summer neighbor commutes to Nantucket in an intercontinental Gulfstream jet.

In light of abundant evidence that context matters, it seems fair to say that Duesenberry's theory rests on a more realistic

"If we take a late retirement and an early death, we'll just squeak by."

model of human nature than Friedman's. It has also been more successful in tracking actual spending. Under the relative-income hypothesis, for example, it is easy to understand why a majority of families experience significant retrenchments in living standards when they retire.[13] Under the permanent-income hypothesis, this observation is a jarring anomaly. And yet Duesenberry's relative-income hypothesis is no longer even mentioned in leading textbooks.

Since rank so often matters for instrumental reasons, caring directly about rank will motivate people to behave in ways that promote their reproductive interests most of the time. So from a

Darwinian perspective, it is perfectly plausible that being informed and motivated by context-sensitive evaluations is just an inherent feature of the human nervous system. This perspective generates detailed hypotheses about the context sensitivity of different types of expenditure. These hypotheses have been investigated more systematically in some domains than in others. Based on what we know so far, however, it is fair to say that available data are largely consistent with these hypotheses.

CHAPTER EIGHT

How Can Middle-Class Families Afford to Keep Up?

With real incomes little higher than they were three decades ago, how are middle-class families able to spend so much more than they used to on houses, cars, watches, interview suits, and gifts? The answer, it turns out, is that they are working every possible angle.

WORKING LONGER HOURS

Women now work an average of approximately two hundred hours more each year than they did in the mid-1970s, and men work an average of roughly one hundred hours more each year.[1] In transnational comparisons, people in countries with high earnings inequality work longer hours than their counterparts in countries with low earnings inequality.[2] Compared to most American cities, earnings inequality is high in the San Francisco Bay Area. About 62 percent of Bay Area couples are dual earners, as compared to the national average of only 57 percent.

REDUCED SAVINGS

Compared to the citizens of other industrial nations, Americans have always had low savings rates. But as income inequality has grown in recent decades, the gap has grown sharply. For much of 1998–1999 — the height of an economic boom of unprecedented duration — the personal savings rate in the United States was actually negative. We were spending more than we earned. Half of the respondents in a survey from that period said they couldn't manage if they had an unexpected bill of $1,000. Another 40 percent said their life savings totaled less than $3,000.[3] Well into the recovery from the 2001 recession, savings rates again became negative during 2005. This was the first time since the Great Depression that the national savings rate was negative for an entire calendar year.

INCREASED INDEBTEDNESS

In 1999, at the height of the economic boom years, American families averaged some $5,000 in revolving credit-card debt, most of it carried at annual interest rates of 17 percent and higher. Here, too, we see suggestions of a link between indebtedness and inequality. For example, despite their higher average incomes, Bay Area families exceeded the average national credit-card debt by more than $1,400 in 1999. Credit counseling services in the Bay Area handled 4,000 cases in 1998, up from only 2,800 cases in 1990.[4] Nationally, one family in sixty-eight filed for bankruptcy in 1998, four times the rate at which families filed for bankruptcy in the early 1980s. Again, this was during an especially prosperous time for the economy. By 2002, the most recent year for which figures are available, the average unpaid credit-card balance for families with at least one card stood at nearly $9,000.

Using U.S. Census data at the county level from 1990 and 2000, Adam Levine and I studied the relationship between increases in inequality and changes in the probability of filing for bankruptcy. We found that even after controlling for income and other known causal factors, bankruptcy filings grew significantly more rapidly in those counties that experienced the greatest growth in income inequality.[5]

LONGER COMMUTES

If you can't afford to live in a good school district in a convenient location, then one solution is to move to a more distant one. Table 2 and the accompanying diagram (figure 16) show the gradient of housing prices versus length of commute to San Francisco from surrounding Bay Area communities.

Similar gradients exist in every community, and these gradients have gotten steeper as income inequality has grown. In general, the more inequality there is in an area, the more expensive the most desirable central locations will be, and the further from the center most middle-income families will feel the need to live.[6] "If you don't want to get yourself in trouble debt-wise you have got to travel," said Sal Gonzales, a thirty-nine-year-old pipe fitter who drives more than an hour each way to his job in San Jose.[7] He sets his alarm clock for 4:30 every morning to get up in time to make that commute. He and his wife, a nurse, earn approximately $100,000 a year. These are not low-income people. Yet they feel they must drive that distance in order to be able pay for the things they feel they need.

Table 2. Price versus length of commute, San Francisco Bay Area

Community	Miles from San Francisco	1998 median house price
Berkeley	12.6	$300,000
Walnut Creek	23.4	$272,750
Petaluma	39.8	$233,000
Antioch	47.2	$155,000
Manteca	75.5	$133,000
Stockton	81.6	$92,500

Source: Curiel, Minton, and McLeod 1999.

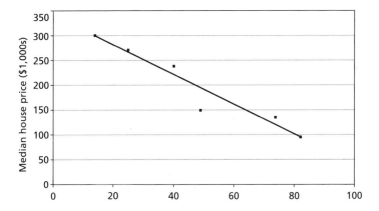

Figure 16. Housing prices versus length of commute.

Elsewhere I have called the relationship between earnings inequality and average commute time "the Aspen effect" (figure 17).[8] In communities where the extremely wealthy congregate, centrally located real estate is so expensive that no middle-class families can afford to live anywhere close by. And yet the wealthy

Figure 17. The Aspen effect. Photograph copyright Gunnar Kullenberg.

residents of communities like Aspen require middle-class people to provide a variety of valued services. The result is that the teachers, restaurant workers, fire fighters, policemen, and other workers who serve these communities must now commute for extremely long distances. Greater Aspen now has a radius well over fifty miles, and the roads leading into the city are clogged for hours each weekday morning and evening. More generally, traffic delays for rush-hour commuters in major U.S. cities roughly tripled between 1983 and 2003.[9] Using census data at the county level from 1990 and 2000, Adam Levine and I found that increases in the proportion of drivers with long commutes were significantly larger in counties with larger increases in income inequality.[10]

GROWING SLEEP DEPRIVATION

With longer hours at work and commuting, Americans are sleeping less than in the past — by some estimates, as much as one to two hours per night less than in the 1960s.[11] In one survey, four in ten adults reported sleeping less than six hours per night.[12] Protracted sleep deprivation has been shown to degrade the immune system. Another concern is that some 100,000 accidents and several thousand deaths per year are caused by drivers who fall asleep at the wheel.[13] Inequality is surely not the sole cause of reduced sleep levels, but by causing increased demands on our time, it is likely to have exacerbated the problem.

PUBLIC SERVICE CUTBACKS

The growing financial distress experienced by middle-class families appears to have reduced their willingness to fund additional public services or even to pay for existing ones. The average voter knows that we all do better if our children attend good schools, if we repair potholes in our roads in a timely fashion, and if our municipal water supplies are free of disease-causing microbes and toxic heavy metals. Yet public budgets have been steadily shrinking in all these areas.

Public school teachers, who earned 118 percent of the average college graduate's salary in 1962, earned only 97 percent as much by 1994.[14] The SAT scores and class rank of persons entering public school teaching have declined steadily during the same period. Class sizes have been growing steadily larger.[15]

Roughly half of the nation's roads are in backlog, meaning that they are overdue for maintenance. Our bridges are in a similar state of disrepair.[16] The deaths of ten motorists when a bridge collapsed over Schoharie Creek on Interstate 90 in New York (figure 18) prompted an emergency inspection of all the state's bridges.[17] More than one-third were found to be structurally

Figure 18. Schoharie Creek Bridge on Interstate 90 in New York State. Photograph courtesy of Scott Keating.

compromised by deferred maintenance. Road maintenance post-poned costs from two to five times as much as maintenance done on schedule.[18] And in the meantime, damaged road surfaces cause an average of $120 in damage each year to every car and truck in the country.[19]

Cutbacks have also occurred in public health. Government inspections of meat processing plants, for example, now occur at only 25 percent of the rate they did in the 1980s, despite the emergence of *E. coli* 0157 and other dangerous new threats.[20] We have been closing drug treatment and prevention centers, despite evidence that we prevent seven dollars in damage for every dollar we spend on these programs.[21] Some forty-five million Americans are now served by municipal water systems from whose antiquated pipes lead and manganese leach into their drinking water.[22]

My argument about cutbacks in basic services raises the following question: Why doesn't the average voter realize that if we elect a Congress that raises taxes to fund basic public services, the extra tax burden won't be very painful? After all, a direct consequence of the tax increase will be an across-the-board reduction in consumption, one result of which should be, according to my argument, that the consumption context will shift, so families won't feel they need to spend as much as before.

I agree that if people actually thought through the consequences of a tax increase in this way, they might indeed be less likely to oppose it. But I also believe that from a psychological perspective, this conceptualization of the problem is totally unnatural (and not just because mainstream economists never call attention to this side effect of tax increases). If I am carrying $5,000 of credit-card debt and thinking about my needs for the next month, and somebody then proposes a tax increase, I am going to say I just can't afford it, even though I am fully cognizant that public services are underfunded. There is just no way in my current circumstances that I could bear a tax increase. It seems far-fetched to imagine that a voter in these circumstances might say, "Yes, raise my taxes, because I know that if we all pay more in taxes, then we'll all have less available for private consumption, and then we won't feel as though we *need* to spend as much on private consumption."

Some twenty-five years ago, my former Cornell colleague Dick Thaler invited me to join him in a wine-tasting class. I declined his invitation, saying that I just didn't want to learn why the six-dollar bottles of wine I felt perfectly happy with at the time were not really as good as I thought. Although Dick is a gifted applied psychologist, he seemed puzzled that anyone would think about the process in those terms. But looking back on it now, I'm still glad to have postponed the effort to educate my palate. While on sabbatical at the Center for Advanced Study in the Behavioral Sciences at Stanford, about to turn fifty and no longer faced with tight budget constraints, I decided the time was ripe to learn more about wine. But drinking first-growth Bordeaux in your early thirties still doesn't strike me as a good plan. What would you have left to look forward to? But most people just don't seem to think about how the kinds of wines they drink today will alter the frame of reference that governs how they feel about the wines they will drink in the future. Nor do most people think about why the burden of a tax increase might be smaller than it first appears, because of its effect on the frame of reference that determines what they feel they need.

CHAPTER NINE

Smart for One, Dumb for All

Context seems to matter in virtually every domain. As noted, however, we are far more sensitive to context in some domains than in others. And that simple fact gives rise to profound distortions in the ways we spend our incomes.

To illustrate, consider the following hypothetical question: Who is happier — a resident of Society A, where everyone lives in a 4,000-square-foot house and drives an hour each way through heavy traffic in order to get to work, or a resident of Society B, where everyone has a 3,000-square-foot house and takes a ten-minute train ride to get to work? (This is something like the actual choice we do confront, since the real resources needed to make larger houses could instead be used to build transit systems that would get people to work quickly.)

Most economists would say you can't answer that question without knowing how people feel about big houses as opposed to short commutes. People who don't mind commuting would prefer the big houses, while others would choose the smaller ones.

It turns out, however, that all available evidence from the behavioral science literature suggests that residents of Society B would be happier. Why? Because the 4,000-square-foot houses in Society A would quickly become the norm for how big a house people feel they need. Similarly, there would be no loss from having the smaller house in Society B, since everyone has a smaller house there. But things are different with commutes. It matters little whether you are the only one who commutes or if everybody commutes. In either case, commutes through heavy traffic reduce well-being. Those who experience such commutes arrive at work with elevated levels of cortisol and other stress hormones in their blood. They're more likely to get into fights with their coworkers when they arrive at work. They're more likely to fight with family members when they get home. They get sick more often in any given month, and die at younger ages.[1] The numbers are strikingly different for those who commute by rail than for those who commute by car through heavy traffic. You don't get used to the latter experience. Nor does the knowledge that others are doing it provide much comfort.

This example illustrates an important general pattern. It portrays a situation in which context matters a lot on one dimension (namely, the size of your house), but matters much less on another (the length of your commute). If you had a 3,000-square-foot house and everyone else had a 4,000-square-foot house, you'd feel uncomfortable about that, in the same way that I would have felt uncomfortable if I had had to live in my Nepal house as a resident of Los Angeles. But a similar asymmetry on the commute dimension would matter far less. The upshot of this asymmetry is that we devote more and more resources to the

Table 3. Choosing between different forms of consumption

	Society A	Society B
1	Everyone lives in 4,000-square-foot houses and has no free time for exercise each day.	Everyone lives in 3,000-square-foot houses and has 45 minutes available for exercise each day.
2	Everyone lives in 4,000-square-foot houses and has time to get together with friends one evening each month.	Everyone lives in 3,000-square-foot houses and has time to get together with friends four evenings each month.
3	Everyone lives in 4,000-square-foot houses and has one week of vacation each year.	Everyone lives in 3,000-square-foot houses and has four weeks of vacation each year.
4	Everyone lives in 4,000-square-foot houses and has a relatively low level of personal autonomy in the workplace.	Everyone lives in 3,000-square-foot houses and has a relatively high level of personal autonomy in the workplace.

context-sensitive category, while we starve the context-insensitive category.

Table 3 lists four similar choices between societies that offer different combinations of material goods and free time to pursue other activities. Each case assumes a specific use of the free time and asks that you imagine it to be one that appeals to you (if not, feel free to substitute some other activity that does). The choice in each case is one between positional consumption (in the form of larger houses) and nonpositional consumption — such as freedom from traffic congestion, time with family and friends, vacation time, and a variety of favorable job characteristics. In each case the evidence suggests that subjective well-being will be higher in the society with a greater balance of nonpositional consumption.[2] And yet in each case the actual trend in U.S. consumption patterns has been in the reverse direction.

The list of consumption items that get short shrift could be extended considerably. Thus we could ask whether living in slightly smaller houses would be a reasonable price to pay for higher air quality, for more urban parkland, for cleaner drinking water, for a reduction in violent crime, or for medical research that would reduce premature death. And in each case the answer would be the same as in the cases we have considered thus far.

My point is not that consumption categories that are less sensitive to context are always preferable to categories that are more sensitive. Indeed, in each case we might envision a minority of rational individuals who might choose Society A over Society B. Some people may simply dislike autonomy on the job, or dislike exercise, or dislike spending time with family and friends.

But if we accept that there is little sacrifice in subjective well-being when all have slightly smaller houses, the real question is whether a rational person could find *some* more productive use for the resources thus saved. Given the absolute sizes of the houses involved in the thought experiments, the answer to this question would seem to be yes.

Our actual spending patterns, however, have been moving in the opposite direction. In recent years, vehicle delays have been growing at about 7 percent per year, meaning that traffic delays double every ten years. There have been increases in the annual number of hours spent at work in the United States during the

last two decades, savings rates are at all-time lows, personal bankruptcy filings are at record levels, and there is at least a wide-
spread perception that employment security and autonomy have
fallen sharply. At the same time, average house size and average
vehicle weight have been growing rapidly.

Why are we doing just the opposite of what the evidence suggests would be best? One of John Kenneth Galbraith's themes in
The Affluent Society was that we are duped by advertisers into
thinking we need more and bigger everything. But if we'd *really*
be happier spending our money differently or taking more time
off, and if it's just the advertisers who are standing in our way,
why not just tune them out? Even when they were very young,
each of my children seemed to have a healthy cynicism about the
claims of cereal manufacturers. Indeed, we all are skeptical about
advertising claims. That doesn't mean we aren't influenced by
them, but if advertising were the only problem, I don't think we
would see a significant imbalance in our spending patterns. To
explain such an imbalance, we need an account that can tell us
why a rational person would spend in the observed ways, even
though it would be better if everyone spent differently.

Let me now attempt to expand on the idea I sketched briefly
in chapter 1. The essence of the idea is captured by the prodi-
gious racks of antlers with which male elk battle one another for
access to females. As the fossil record shows, these antlers, which
now span five feet or more, started out much smaller. But in
every generation, mutant elks with slightly bigger antlers won
more fights and hence passed more of their genes for big antlers
into the next generation. Antlers, in short, became the focus of a
runaway evolutionary arms race.

Is that a problem? In densely wooded areas, one disadvantage is that the bearer of broader antlers is severely handicapped in his efforts to flee from wolves and other predators. Suppose elks could take a vote on a proposal to reduce the breadth of each animal's rack of antlers by half. If they had any sense, they'd all vote yes, because the fights would still be decided in precisely the same way as before, and yet each animal would enjoy increased security from predators. In the contests for access to mates, it's the relative size of an animal's antlers that counts, not how big they are in absolute terms. But when fleeing from predators in densely wooded areas, greater absolute antler width is a serious handicap.

It might seem that this is a problem that would solve itself, since a mutant elk with smaller antlers would enjoy relative immunity from predators. True enough, but such an animal also wouldn't leave any offspring, and in the Darwinian contest, that's the only payoff that counts. To escape to live to be an old elk doesn't really matter much if the animal doesn't leave any offspring. Oversized antlers belong to a class of traits and behaviors that I have described as smart for one, dumb for all.[3] They are a simple consequence of a positional arms race.

We see a precisely analogous problem in the choice about housing. I can choose the size of my house, but I can't choose the size of your house. We might say that if we each had a smaller house, or if we each postponed the upgrade from 3,000 to 4,000 square feet and used the money in a different way, that would be good. But I as an individual have no power to do that. I can choose the size of my own house and that's pretty much it.

This example encapsulates my diagnosis of the problem. It's not that we're dupes of the advertisers; it's not that we're manipulated by special interests; it's not that we're those frail, irrational creatures that social critics often make us out to be. Rather it's that many of the decisions we confront are like those confronting participants in a military arms race. Countries don't buy bombs because they're stupid; they buy them because it's bad not to have bombs when the other side has bombs. But although it is not stupid for individual nations in that situation to buy bombs, it can be extremely beneficial for them to forge agreements to limit the number of bombs they buy — provided each side can police the agreement and make sure that the other abides by it.

Similarly, although the evidence suggests that we would be happier if we *all* bought smaller houses and cars, and spent what we saved in the process on a variety of less conspicuous forms of consumption, that is not an option open to individual consumers. Again, the problem is that each family can control how much it spends, not how much others spend.

Behaviors that are smart for one, dumb for all, actually have a long history in economic analysis. Such behaviors are often observed in situations characterized as "tragedies of the commons." An example is overharvesting in common fisheries, which occurs because no individual has an incentive to limit her own personal catch in the present for the sake of leaving enough fish to sustain the fishery (which would benefit everyone in the future). Overgrazing of common pastureland is another example. Or suppose everybody stands up to get a better view. Nobody sees any better than if everybody had remained seated. There are thousands of familiar examples. Smart for one, dumb for all is neither a new nor a controversial idea.

Yet there's a very influential school in our political debate whose position is that there's essentially no such thing as the tragedy of the commons. In this view, the best outcomes are always and everywhere the ones that result when people are free as individuals to do exactly as they please. The question for historians to answer will be: How did this group get to be so influential? What a curious position to hold in view of all the evidence we have. How, historians will ask, did people who denied the existence of tragedies of the commons ever get anyone to take them seriously? I don't have a good answer to that.

CHAPTER TEN

Looking Ahead

Evidence suggests that, relative to the mix of goods that would maximize our health and happiness, we spend too much on context-sensitive goods and too little on goods that are relatively insensitive to context. Looking ahead, there is little reason to think the spending imbalance will cure itself and considerable reason to expect it to grow worse.

The imbalance has been growing because of the tendency for income and wealth to become more concentrated among top earners. This tendency, in turn, owes much to the spread and intensification of what Philip Cook and I have called "winner-take-all markets."[1] These are markets in which small differences in performance translate into extremely large differences in reward.

Such markets have long been familiar in entertainment and sports. The best soprano may be only marginally better than the second-best, but in a world in which most people listen to music on compact discs, there is little need for the second-best. In such a world, the best soprano may earn a seven-figure annual salary while the second-best struggles to get by. In similar fashion, new technologies allow us to clone the services of the most talented performers in a growing number of occupations, thereby enabling them to serve ever broader and more lucrative markets.

The market for tax advice, for example, was once served almost exclusively by a large army of local practitioners but is increasingly served by the developers of a small handful of software programs. Scores of programs competed for reviewer approval in the early stages of this transition. But once opinion leaders anointed Intuit's TurboTax and Kiplinger's TaxCut as the most comprehensive, user-friendly programs, most competing programs quickly disappeared from view.

A constellation of factors helps us understand why similar shakeouts have occurred in industry after industry. The information revolution has made us more aware of product quality differences than ever and puts us in direct contact with the world's best suppliers. Sharply reduced transportation costs and tariff barriers enable these suppliers to ship their products to us more cheaply than before. Research and development costs and other fixed costs now constitute a larger share of total costs, making it harder for small producers to achieve efficient scale.

But although technology has conferred greater leverage on key actors in almost every arena, the causal chain between greater leverage and greater inequality would be incomplete without an additional link: more open competition in labor markets. A case in point is the time profile of player salary growth in major league baseball. With the arrival of national TV broadcasts in the 1950s, baseball players began performing before thirty million fans instead of just thirty thousand, an enormous increase in their economic leverage. And yet the salaries of baseball players remained more or less static in real terms during the ensuing two decades. Almost the entire infusion of new revenue attributable to televised games went to team owners, almost none to the players themselves. Players were in an extremely weak bargaining position then, because they were the property of whichever team drafted them. There was essentially no competition in the market for established major league baseball players.

That all changed dramatically with the abolition of the reserve clause, the result of court decisions in 1975 and 1976. Suddenly players were free to sell their services to the highest bidder. And only then did the real runaway increases in baseball players' salaries begin. The leverage made possible by television was a necessary condition for today's multi-million-dollar contracts. But it was not sufficient. There also had to be competitive bidding for players, and we didn't see that until the late 1970s.

A similar chain of events has played out in the market for CEOs. The leaders of large corporations have always had enormous economic leverage. Even during the 1920s, a slightly better set of decisions by GM's CEO would have translated into millions of dollars of extra profit each year. With the broader scope of today's markets, the economic leverage of CEOs is greater still. But as in baseball, economic leverage alone is insufficient to generate extremely high salaries. There must also be open competition in executive labor markets. Until very recently, however, it was rare for CEOs to take over without having spent almost their entire careers with the same corporation. So we didn't really have an effectively competitive market for CEO talent.

That all has changed now. More and more, we see firms bidding top executives away from other firms in the same industry, and even from firms in completely unrelated industries. A celebrated case in point was IBM's dramatically successful turnaround, which began when the company hired RJR Nabisco's CEO, Lou Gerstner. Decades ago, the idea of a tobacco CEO taking over a large computer company would have been unthinkable. Today such moves are not at all unusual. If you know how to do finance, if you know how to do marketing, if you can motivate people, then it doesn't matter whether you know all about mainframe computers. You have tech people for that.

Of course, not all of the increase in income inequality that we've seen in recent decades is a consequence of the growing importance of winner-take-all markets. Some has resulted from the fact that the economic return to having a college education has risen since the 1980s. In the 1970s, many economists suggested that it was no longer worthwhile to get a college education, but that's clearly not the case today.

But the increased return to higher education is only part of the story. No matter how you slice the data, the pattern of inequality growth is almost exactly the same. If you look only at college graduates, for example, the basic pattern is that those at the bottom of the earnings ladder have gained almost no ground since 1980, those in the middle have gained only slightly, and those at the top have experienced extremely rapid earnings growth. The same is true of authors, real-estate agents, and physics majors. Within almost every group, the pattern is the same as the one we see for the economy as a whole. Top performers are succeeding spectacularly well, people in the middle are only a little ahead of where they were, and those at the bottom are holding roughly even.

Others have suggested that increased inequality is largely the result of unskilled workers' wages being driven down by competition from foreign labor. Obviously that's been important in some occupations. But we see the same pattern of inequality growth when we look at occupations that are largely unaffected by foreign competition. Phil Cook and I were surprised, for example, that the pattern of inequality change is much the same for dentists as for other occupations, even though dentists are not affected by foreign competition at all (with the possible exception of those who practice in a handful of border cities).

Dentistry didn't sound like a typical winner-take-all market to us, either. But in fact if you look at the income distribution for dentists, those in the bottom quintile are earning somewhat less than they did twenty years ago, those in the middle are earning about the same, and those at the top are earning spectacularly more than before. It is not that the top earners are filling more cavities than the others. Rather, they are for the most part successful entrepreneurs in the booming business of cosmetic dentistry.

This particular market illustrates how winner-take-all processes often turn out to be mutually reinforcing. As the top earners in other fields earn more, their demand for premium cosmetic dentistry grows. And the premium salaries of the leading cosmetic dentists similarly fuel demand for the services of leading performers in other arenas.

The kind of degree you earned also affects your earnings prospects. If you graduated in a technical field during the last twenty years, you're probably doing better than if you graduated in the humanities. Compared to computer science majors, humanities majors have fared poorly in the job market of late. But if we look within humanities majors, we see the same pattern

"English lit—how about you?"

as for other groups. Some humanities majors are doing spectacularly well. The ones in the middle haven't gained much ground, and the ones at the bottom have gained hardly any.

These are long-run forces I've been describing. It's anybody's guess what will happen to the economy in the near term. But longer term, technology will continue driving changes in the distributions of income and wealth, and changes in these distributions will continue to drive changes in spending. I don't see anything to indicate that winner-take-all technologies have played out. In every product and service category, some producers have always been much better than others, and some buyers have always been willing to pay more for high quality than others.

Technology will continue to allow the best producers to extend their reach. And it will continue to do a better job of putting high-income buyers in touch with producers who can better serve them. The task of matching these players up can only get easier in the future.

In short, many of the forces that have been causing inequality to grow seem to be gathering steam. The explosive growth of online book sales by Amazon.com has slowed from its peak, but the company's online sales in other markets have more than made up the difference. It and other online retailers continue to displace traditional small-scale retail operations. As these processes unfold, the concentration of income and wealth at the top will continue to grow, and with it the imbalance in our current spending patterns.

My point is not that we haven't all benefited greatly from the processes that are creating the spectacular gains for the people at the top. The additional wealth generated by technical change and increased competition is more than enough to reinvigorate our schools, fix our roads and bridges, provide universal health insurance, clean up the environment, and more generally to boost all those consumption categories that the evidence suggests are getting short shrift at the moment. Shifting our spending patterns in these ways would entail little or no psychological penalty, if we all did it. All it would entail is postponing the upgrade of the mansion to the next larger size, postponing the upgrade from the five-thousand-dollar grill to the next larger size, and so on. Absent any collective commitment to postpone those spending upgrades, however, what's in store for us is more of the same. As incomes continue to grow at the top and stagnate elsewhere, we will see even more of our national income devoted to luxury goods, the main effect of which will be to raise the bar that defines what counts as luxury.

Out of curiosity, I ordered the Frontgate catalog one year after I went shopping for a new gas grill, just to see how what the company had on offer had changed. At the high end, it was offering the same Viking Frontgate Professional model as before, but this time the basic unit was embedded in a fixed island that a contractor would construct in your backyard. The ancillary range-top burners in the new unit were set well off to the left side. Still further to the left, there was a tiled bar with a handsome canvas umbrella, and off to the right there was a wood-fired pizza oven. The ensemble was offered for $13,769.

More expensive units are now available. One has a lobster steamer and an electric 35,000-BTU wok built into it. (Why use only 15,000 BTUs to sear the flavor in when you could use 35,000?) Another is the $35,000 Talos Outdoor Cooking Suite. Also sold by Frontgate, it "features a searing station with a restaurant-style griddle, a hardwood cutting board, two side burners to heat sauces, a warming drawer, 3/8-inch-thick cooking grates, a 16,000-BTU ceramic infrared rotisserie, a bartender module with a sink and a nine-volt electronic ignition system."[2]

It would be nice to have one of these outdoor grills. But if we all postponed the upgrade, we could spend the same money in ways that would make each and every one of us happier with our situation. That's the basic message from the literature on human subjective well-being.

CHAPTER ELEVEN

Lessons for Public Policy

Can we draw from this discussion any useful lessons for public policy? Evidence from the human happiness literature strongly suggests that our current expenditures fail to take full advantage of the opportunities available to us. Roughly speaking, the problem is that we work too many hours, save too little, and spend too much of our incomes on goods that confer little additional satisfaction when all have more of them.

Historically, some societies responded to essentially the same mix of problems by adopting sumptuary laws. These laws were complete failures.[1] The moment gold buttons were outlawed, people immediately switched to fancy carved ivory ones. When lace was outlawed, people turned to imported silks. My favorite example was the attempt in medieval Florence to outlaw the multicourse meals that had grown ever more expensive as people began hosting increasingly elaborate dinner parties. This particular sumptuary law limited hosts to serving only a single-course meal. Shortly after its enactment, clever chefs created the meat and pasta torte, a dish that often took even longer to prepare than the multicourse meals it replaced.

The general rule with proscriptive regulation of this sort is that if you ban one activity, people quickly switch to a close substitute. The same is true with respect to the levy of luxury taxes on selected products. In the early 1990s, for example, the U.S. government levied luxury taxes on planes, yachts, and certain cars, a principal effect of which was that consumers switched to untaxed substitutes, often with undesired side effects. A large demand shift toward untaxed second-hand yachts and other substitutes, for example, led to major employment cutbacks in many American shipbuilding companies.

If the problem is that we work too hard and save too little because of competitive pressures to bid for houses in the best school districts, the only effective policy levers will be those that alter spending incentives in more general ways. One escape from the positional arms race might be a legal requirement that each family save at least a threshold fraction of its earnings each year.

In one sense, the Social Security program can be interpreted as just such a requirement. The payroll tax, in effect, renders 12 percent of our gross labor earnings unavailable for the bidding war for a house in a better school district or to spend on a more expensive interview suit. Of course, Social Security is not a savings program at all, but rather a transfer from workers to retirees. But from the perspective of any individual, it is the functional equivalent of a savings plan.

Mandating higher savings is a form of intervention that recalls the heavy-handed command-and-control regulations employed in the early years of the battle against environmental pollution. We have too much pollution simply because polluting is more attractive to individuals than to society as a whole. The most efficient way to attack the problem, economists argued, was to levy charges on those whose activities generate pollution. Recent experience has shown that effluent taxes and permit fees have enabled us to reduce pollution at only a fraction of the cost formerly incurred under command-and-control regulation.[2]

Similarly, if our problem is that certain forms of private consumption currently seem more attractive to individuals than to society as a whole, the simplest solution is to make those forms less attractive by taxing them. Shifting to a progressive consumption tax could change our incentives in just this way.

Proposals to tax consumption raise the specter of forbidding complexity — of having to save receipts for each purchase, of endless bickering over which products are to be exempt, and so on. Yet a system of progressive consumption taxation could be achieved by a simple one-line amendment to the federal tax code — namely, by making savings exempt from tax. This is so because the amount a family consumes each year is just the difference between the amount it earns and the amount it saves. Administratively, a progressive consumption tax is thus essentially similar to our current progressive income tax. A family would report its income to the IRS each year, just as it does now. It would also report the amount saved during the year, as participants in 401(k) and other retirement savings programs currently do. Its tax would then depend on its total consumption, which is the difference in these two amounts.

The following example illustrates how the tax might work for a family of four if the standard deduction were $7,500 per person. With a total standard deduction of $30,000 per year, the family's taxable consumption would be calculated as its income minus $30,000 minus its savings minus its tax. A family whose income was no more than $30,000 plus the amount it saved would thus owe no

Table 4. Tax rates on taxable consumption

Taxable Consumption	Marginal Tax Rate (percent)
0–$39,999	20
$40,000–49,999	22
$50,000–59,999	24
$60,000–69,999	26
$70,000–79,999	28
$80,000–89,999	30
$90,000–99,999	32
$100,000–129,999	34
$130,000–159,999	38
$160,000–189,999	42
$190,000–219,999	46
$220,000–249,999	50
$250,000–499,000	60
$500,000–999,999	80
$1,000,000–1,999,999	100
$2,000,000–3,999,999	150
$4,000,000+	200

tax at all under this plan. Because high-income families save a substantially higher proportion of their incomes than low-income families, maintaining the current tax burden across income levels would require top marginal tax rates on consumption that are much higher than the current top marginal tax rates on income. In the illustrative rate schedule shown in table 4, families with positive taxable consumption are taxed at an initial rate of 20 percent, which then rises gradually as taxable consumption increases.

Table 5. Illustrative income, savings, and tax values under a
progressive consumption tax

Income	Savings	Taxable Consumption	Tax
$30,000	$1,500	0	0
$50,000	$3,000	$14,167	$2,833
$100,000	$10,000	$49,836	$10,164
$150,000	$20,000	$81,538	$18,462
$200,000	$40,000	$104,328	$25,672
$500,000	$120,000	$258,000	$92,000
$1,000,000	$300,000	$458,000	$212,000
$1,500,000	$470,000	$646,000	$354,000
$2,500,000	$800,000	$1,029,900	$667,100
$3,500,000	$1,200,000	$1,316,400	$953,600
$20,000,000	$10,000,000	$4,444,267	$5,525,733

Note: The income figures in this table are illustrative. The savings figures
are assumed, but they reflect the reality that higher-income people save at
higher rates than lower-income people do.

The top rate of 200 percent shown in the table means that
someone who was already spending more than four million dollars per year would need three dollars of additional income to
support each additional dollar of consumption. Given this rate
schedule, table 5 shows how much tax families with different
income and savings levels would pay.

It might seem that a top marginal rate of 200 percent on additional consumption at the highest levels would severely compromise the ability of many wealthy Americans to support the standard of living to which they have grown accustomed. But what sorts of sacrifices, exactly, would living with this tax entail? Many top earners currently spend their marginal consumption dollars in ways that, from the perspective of the nonrich, at least, appear to generate little impact. Consider, for example, Patek Philippe's Calibre '89, perhaps the most remarkably elaborate and accurate mechanical watch ever built. With its $2.7 million price tag, this particular timepiece is purchased only by persons of extreme wealth. Among its many features is a "tourbillon" — a gyroscope that turns about once each minute, whose purpose is to offset the distortionary effects of Earth's gravitational field. Yet despite its formidable engineering wizardry, the Calibre '89 is actually less accurate than a battery-powered quartz watch costing less than $20. Earth's gravitational field, it turns out, doesn't affect the accuracy of an electronic watch.

Accurate or not, top-of-the line mechanical wristwatches are selling briskly. On a recent field trip to New York City, for example, I learned that a Patek Philippe watch priced at $45,000 is available only on back order, and that sales of watches costing more than $2,000 are growing at almost 13 percent a year. The men who purchase these mechanical wristwatches (women almost never buy them) often own several, which confronts them with a problem: Although the watches are self-winding, they will stop if put aside for a few days. So the owner of several of these watches must often reset each one before wearing it.

One could hardly expect men of means to tolerate such a problem for long. And sure enough, there is now a ready solution. On display in the Asprey & Garrard showrooms on Fifth Avenue in Manhattan, discerning buyers will find a finely tooled calfskin-leather-covered box with a golden clasp, whose doors open to reveal six mechanical wrists that rotate just often enough to keep the mechanical wristwatches they hold running smoothly. The price? Only $5,700. For those who find that box too expensive, Asprey & Garrard also offers a value model with only three wrists and priced at just $3,000.

Among America's wealthiest taxpayers, a progressive consumption tax would provide powerful incentives to spend less on wristwatches and build smaller mansions than they would otherwise. How big a sacrifice would that be? If one's goal were simply to have a watch that meets the standards of one's peer group, that goal would not be compromised at all if everyone in each group spent a little less. And the same is true in the case of house size. Indeed, it is easy to imagine that the wealthy might actually be *happier* if they all had smaller houses. Just think of how many staff members you'd need underfoot just to keep things functioning in a 70,000-square-foot house.

The progressive consumption tax illustrated in this example is different from other consumption taxes such as the value-added tax or the national sales tax, which are levied at the same rate no matter how much a family consumes. Those taxes have been criticized as regressive because of the positive link between savings rates and household income (or, put another way, because those with lower income tend to spend a larger percentage of their income than do those with higher income). Under the proposed tax, escalating marginal tax rates on consumption, coupled with the large standard deduction, ensure that total tax as a proportion of income would rise steadily with income, even though the assumed savings rate is sharply higher for high-income families.

Consumption taxation has been proposed before.[3] Authors of earlier proposals have focused on the fact that because a progressive consumption tax exempts income from taxation until it is spent, it would shift incentives in favor of savings and investment.[4] But a progressive consumption tax would also reinforce other motives for saving, such as the desire to hedge against the possibility of becoming disabled and the desire to leave bequests to heirs and charities. Moral hazard and adverse selection make private savings more attractive than commercial insurance as a hedge against lost earning power, and a steeply progressive consumption tax lowers the cost of self-insuring. It also lowers the cost of leaving bequests to heirs and charities. So on these additional grounds as well, a progressive consumption tax could be expected to stimulate higher savings.

Yet another channel through which such a tax would limit current consumption is by directly constraining the expenditures of high-income individuals who now consume most or all of their after-tax incomes. Consider, for example, a person who currently earns $3.5 million a year and consumes all his after-tax income (say, $2,100,000 per year). Under the illustrative tax rates shown in table 4, the most this person could consume and still cover his tax bill out of current income would be $1,733,120, a reduction of more than 17 percent.

If the tax affected spending directly for any or all of the reasons mentioned, it would also affect spending indirectly. Each individual's spending, after all, constitutes part of the frame of reference that influences what others spend. And given how strongly context affects demand, the indirect effects of a progressive consumption tax promise to be considerably larger than the direct effects.

Switching to a progressive consumption tax would also create a potential revenue source for funding equity accounts to supplement Social Security payments during retirement. For unlike higher top marginal rates on income, higher top marginal rates on consumption not only would not limit incentives to save and invest, but would actually increase them.

It might seem natural to worry that a tax that limits consumption might lead to recession and unemployment. This is not a serious long-run concern, however, because money that is not spent on consumption would be saved and invested. The result is that some of the people who are now employed to produce consumption goods would instead be employed to produce capital goods — which, in the long run, would increase the economy's productive capacity.

In the short run, if a recession should occur, a more powerful fiscal remedy would be available under a consumption tax than is currently available under the income tax. Under the current tax structure, a standard textbook remedy for recession is a temporary income tax cut. The problem with this remedy, however, is that those who remain employed have a strong incentive to save their tax cuts as a hedge against the possibility of becoming unemployed. A temporary consumption tax cut would not entail this difficulty, since the only way consumers could benefit from it would be by actually spending more money now. Transition problems could be minimized by phasing in the program gradually — with phased increases in the amount of savings a family could exempt and phased increases in the highest marginal tax rates.

I cannot help noting the striking contrast between the proposals I have just described and the policies of the George W. Bush administration, which has enacted the largest ever cut in our income taxes, most of it targeted to families with the highest earnings. Facing enormous federal budget deficits at a time when we are not paying teachers enough, not repairing our roads, bridges, and municipal water supply systems, and not inspecting the meat we eat, can multi-trillion-dollar tax cuts really be a sensible policy? At a time when top earners have been reaping virtually all the fruits of the nation's economic growth, can targeting more than 50 percent of the benefits of these tax cuts to the top 5 percent of earners really be a sensible step?

Cynics explain the apparent anomaly by saying that the wealthy have captured the political process in Washington and are exploiting it to their own advantage. This explanation makes sense, however, only if those in power have an extremely naive understanding of their own interests. A careful reading of the evidence suggests that even the wealthy have been made worse off, on balance, by recent tax cuts. The private benefits of these cuts have been much smaller, and their indirect costs much larger, than many recipients appear to have anticipated.

On the benefit side, tax cuts have led the wealthy to buy larger houses, in the seemingly plausible expectation that doing so would make them happier. But as we have seen, available evidence suggests that when everyone's house grows larger, the primary effect is merely to redefine what qualifies as an acceptable dwelling. So, although the recent tax cuts have enabled the wealthy to buy more and bigger things, these purchases appear to have had little impact on their happiness. As the economist Richard Layard has written, "In a poor country, a man proves to his wife that he loves her by giving her a rose, but in a rich country, he must give a dozen roses."[5]

On the cost side of the ledger, the federal budget deficits created by the recent tax cuts have had serious consequences, even for the wealthy. These deficits will exceed three hundred billion dollars for each of the next six years, according to projections by the nonpartisan Congressional Budget Office. The most widely reported consequences of the deficits have been cuts in government programs that serve the nation's poorest families. And since the wealthy are well represented in our political system, their favored programs may seem safe from the budget ax. Wealthy families have further insulated themselves by living in gated communities and sending their children to private schools. Yet such steps go only so far.

For example, deficits have led to cuts in federal financing for basic scientific research, even as the United States' share of global patents granted continues to decline. Such cuts threaten the very basis of our long-term economic prosperity. As Senator Pete Domenici, Republican of New Mexico, said: "We thought we'd keep the high-end jobs, and others would take the low-end jobs. We're now on track to a second-rate economy and a second-rate country."[6]

Citing revenue shortfalls, the nation postpones maintenance of its streets and highways, even though, as noted, doing so means having to spend two to five times as much on repairs in the long run. In the short run, bad roads cause thousands of accidents each year, many of them fatal. Poor people die in these accidents, but so do rich people. When a pothole destroys a tire and wheel, replacements cost only $63 for a Ford Escort but $1,569 for a Porsche 911.

Deficits have also compromised the nation's security. In 2004, for example, the Bush administration reduced financing by 8 percent for the Energy Department's program to secure inadequately guarded nuclear stockpiles in the former Soviet Union. Sam Nunn, now retired from the Senate, heads a private foundation whose mission is to raise private donations to expedite this effort. And despite the rational fear that terrorists may try to detonate a nuclear bomb in an American city, most cargo containers continue to enter the nation's ports without inspection.

Large federal budget deficits and low household savings rates have also forced our government to borrow more than $650 billion each year, primarily from China, Japan, and South Korea. These loans must be repaid in full, with interest. The resulting financial burden, plus the risks associated with increased international monetary instability, fall disproportionately on the rich.

Moralists often urge the wealthy to imagine how easily their lives could have turned out differently, to adopt a more generous posture toward those less prosperous. But top earners might also wish to consider evidence that their own families would have been better off, in purely practical terms, had it not been for the tax cuts of recent years.

The Bush tax cuts were sold with slogans such as "It's your money, and you know how to spend it better than any bureaucrat does." Such statements have obvious rhetorical force. Yet the gains promised by tax-cutters are completely illusory. Indeed, the primary effect of the tax cuts will be to worsen an already serious imbalance in the overall mix of things we buy. With more cash in their pockets, top earners will demand still bigger houses and cars. And increased spending at the top will spawn additional spending by others further down.

Ardent tax-cut proponents will respond: "So what? If top earners want to spend the wealth they have generated on bigger houses and cars, why should Congress second-guess them? And if middle-class families can't afford to keep up, why can't they just summon the will to live within their means?"

But here again we have powerful rhetoric that breaks down on closer scrutiny. As we have seen, the problem confronting a family is like the one confronting a participant in a military arms race. It can choose how much of its own money to spend, but it cannot choose how much others spend. A middle-income family that buys a smaller-than-average house typically must send its children to below-average schools. Buying a smaller-than-average vehicle means greater risk of dying in an accident. Spending less — on bombs or on personal consumption — frees up money for other pressing uses, but only if everyone does it.

The persistent budget deficits that stretch before us will continue to gut public services once considered essential. At a time when we are wealthier than ever, does it really make sense to be closing our public libraries on Sundays?

Proponents of smaller government argue that if we let the government spend more money, more will be wasted. This is true, of course, but only in the trivial sense that there would be more of everything the government does — good and bad — if public spending were higher.

The solution favored by many opponents of government waste, epitomized in the Proposition 13 movement in California, is to starve the government. But, as Californians have belatedly recognized, this remedy is like trying to starve a tapeworm by not eating. Residents of the Golden State once proudly sent their children to the nation's best public schools. Now California's public schools are among the nation's worst.

The question, then, isn't whether bureaucrats know best how to spend our money. Rather, it's "How much of *our* money do *we* want to spend on public services?" We could adopt a progressive consumption tax whose revenues could be used to help restore public services that deliver good value for our money. Or we could continue the Bush program of tax cuts that will help fuel an already intense consumption spiral.

Do we want to spend our money on better teachers, better roads, and enhanced national security? Or do we want to spend it on more expensive watches, more elaborate gas grills, and bigger mansions? That's a choice we must make in the political arena. Tired slogans about government waste won't help us make this decision more intelligently. We need to have an open discussion about what our tax rates and public spending policies ought to be. Sadly, we haven't been able to have that discussion in the current environment.

If income inequality is not the only source of the problems I have discussed here, it surely contributes to most of them. If someone could show that we needed to have high inequality to achieve the growth that we have had over the last one hundred years, then we would confront a difficult trade-off. But the literature on growth and inequality provides scant evidence that we actually face such a trade-off. On the contrary, recent work in this area suggests that countries with high inequality grow more slowly, on the average, than countries with low inequality. And over time, countries tend to grow more rapidly during periods of low inequality than they do during periods of high inequality.[7]

CHAPTER TWELVE

Reflections

Incomes have been largely static during recent decades except for those of earners in the top quintile. The real incomes of the top 1 percent have tripled since 1979, while those higher up the income ladder have enjoyed far more spectacular gains. CEOs of America's largest companies, who earned 42 times as much as the average worker as recently as 1980, now earn more than 500 times as much.

As a general rule, a family's total lifetime spending tracks its total lifetime income closely. Because top earners in the United States now earn so much more than they used to, their spending levels have risen accordingly. I don't mean that as a moral indictment of them. That's just what every group does when it earns more money. Poor families spend more when they earn more. So do middle-class families. And so do the rich.

Although many of the things the rich buy may seem spectacularly wasteful to people in the middle class, we must bear in mind that consumption standards are local. Many of the things that middle-income consumers buy in this country would seem spectacularly wasteful to most of the inhabitants of the planet. For example, if my friends from the village where I taught in Nepal were to see the house I now live in, they'd think I'd taken leave of my senses. It's a nice house, yet by my own local standards, it wouldn't even raise an eyebrow. To a Nepali's eyes, however, it would seem like a palace.

The increased spending by top earners has changed the frame of reference that shapes the spending decisions of those just below them. So the near-rich are spending more, too, and their spending in turn has altered the relevant frame of reference for others just below them, and so on, all the way down the income ladder.

Has rising inequality harmed the middle class? I believe that the evidence is clear that it has. To send its children to a school of average quality, the median household must spend considerably more than in decades past, even though its real purchasing power has scarcely grown.

My point isn't that life overall has become more miserable for the middle class. Medical technology continues to improve, for example, and that benefits everyone. Many children who died from leukemia twenty-five years ago are now being cured of it. My message is rather that life for people in the middle is more difficult than it would have been if income growth had been more balanced in recent decades.

Utilitarians have long argued against income inequality on the grounds that the marginal utility of income is typically smaller for a wealthy person than for a poor person. In their view, transferring one thousand dollars of income from a rich person to a poor person is justified because the extra happiness experienced when the poor person receives the money would far outweigh the decline in happiness when the rich person gives it up. Although some have objected to this argument, saying that no one knows for sure how gains and losses affect the well-being of people in different circumstances, most people accept that an extra dollar generally meets more pressing demands for a poor person than for a rich person.

The utilitarian argument for limiting inequality is strengthened considerably by the observation that demand for many of the things we buy is driven in part by their function as signals — both of ability and of the importance of specific relationships. "It's all about who has what," said William Unger, a Madison Avenue retailer, as he described a conversation he had overheard between two men, each wearing a five-figure wristwatch. "The friend sees his friend has a [Patek Philippe] Pagoda, and these are people who have a certain intuitiveness; they know how much things cost. They ascertain what a guy's capability or monetary status is by looking at his watch. They know if he's a player. Or they think they know."[1]

In an environment in which signal strength depends on relative expenditure, little would be sacrificed if all spent less. If the only reason you need a larger house or a more expensive watch is to signal where you stand in the social order, then all could gain by creating an incentive to keep score by other means — say, by how big an asset account you can accumulate or by how much you contribute to charity, rather than by how big a mansion you can build. Those would be far more socially productive ways of keeping score. You're not going to eliminate the impulse to keep score. But you can make it less costly, in the same way that putting helmets on hockey players makes it less costly for them to compete all out in a hockey game.

Some have expressed concern that if we try to curb status seeking by reducing inequality through the tax system, people might just create other ways to compete for status that are even more costly than the ones we have now. That certainly is a logical possibility. If we had a 100 percent marginal tax rate on earned income, nobody would work at all, and then people would definitely focus on other ways to compete. But relatively modest increases in top marginal income tax rates, or a switch to a progressive consumption tax, would be unlikely to drive competition into new arenas. What drives the current competition is the desire to attain high relative purchasing power. Even with higher tax rates, people will still want relatively big houses.

A progressive consumption tax wouldn't change the fundamental impulse to buy nice things. But it would give everyone an incentive to join you in cutting back. In the process, it would greatly reduce the waste that now occurs from acting on that impulse. Paul Allen, the cofounder of Microsoft, lives in a 70,000-square-foot house. It would not be a great sacrifice for him or others if all people at that income level lived instead in 50,000-square-foot houses. That's still more house than they can really manage to use on a day-to-day basis. After all, a 50,000-square-foot house is more than six times as big as the house shown in figure 19.

The tax remedy I favor obviously is not the only solution that has been proposed for the problems confronting us. Many have argued, for example, that voluntary private action can be an effective substitute for collective efforts to change our incentives. Perhaps the most familiar example in this vein is the voluntary simplicity movement. Leaders of this movement advocate simpler styles of life. Cut back your hours at work, live in smaller

Figure 19. 8,000-square-foot house. Photograph courtesy of John Henry Design International, Inc.

dwellings, buy less expensive cars, take vacations closer to home, eat simpler meals at home with friends rather than at expensive restaurants.[2] That kind of advice, if followed by a circle of friends earning $150,000 per couple, would often yield a clear improvement in the day-to-day experience of life.

But if you're trying to raise a family of four on $30,000 a year and cut back your hours in an attempt to lead a less stressful life, which purchases do you reduce? You're already living in a school district that's not as good as the one you want your kids to be in. You're already driving a fifteen-year-old car. You're already taking your lunch to work. You don't really have a lot of things that you can cut back easily without compromising high-priority items from the list of things you care about.

The voluntary simplicity authors have been at this for more than twenty years now, arguing that people ought to cut back, and yet every year the savings rate goes down and the number of hours worked goes up. It may be that they are making a difference — that things might have been even worse except for their efforts. But even if so, the voluntary simplicity movement will not be a sufficient response in the long term. The problem is that our current spending patterns are smart for one, dumb for all. If cutting back isn't smart for one, then we're not going to see many people cut back.

In our current political environment, the idea of adopting a progressive consumption tax might seem little more than a political pipe dream. Yet the features of this particular tax have demonstrated their appeal not only to liberals but also to staunch conservatives. For example, in response to an article I wrote about this tax proposal several years ago, I got a very friendly letter from Milton Friedman, the conservative Nobel laureate. He included a reprint of an article he had published in the *American Economic Review* in 1943, in which he had advocated a progressive consumption tax as by far the most efficient way to pay for the war effort. Of course, he challenged my view that we need to raise more revenue for public services at the moment. But the point of his article was that if we did want to raise more revenue, a progressive consumption tax would be the best way to do it. And that point is no less valid today than it was in 1943.

There actually was a tax bill very much like the one I propose introduced in the Senate in 1995. The economist Larry Seidman has written extensively about this proposal.[3] It was called the Unlimited Savings Allowance tax, or USA tax, and its sponsors were Sam Nunn, the Democrat from Georgia, and Pete Domenici, the Republican from New Mexico. It was a serious proposal. Shortly after its introduction, however, budget battles erupted between the Republican Congress and President Clinton, and it never came to the floor for a vote. But no one argued at the time that it was a radical idea. On the contrary, it was a sensible proposal with solid bipartisan sponsorship.

Our political discourse has coarsened considerably in the years since Senators Nunn and Domenici introduced their progressive consumption tax bill. Politicians who introduced a similar proposal today could be sure that opponents would run thirty-second ads attacking them for believing that bureaucrats in Washington know best how to spend people's hard-earned dollars. Such ads have sunk more than a few promising political careers. So if proponents of rational tax reform have sought to remain in the shadows of late, that is hardly surprising.

From a reformer's perspective, perhaps the single most discouraging development in the current policy debate has been the apparent breadth of the public support for President Bush's proposal for permanent repeal of the estate tax. This tax, which the president calls the "death tax," currently affects less than 1 percent of all estates, and the lion's share of its revenue comes from estates larger than five million dollars. Yet even among the poorest voters, whose family members face virtually no risk of ever having to pay this tax, opinion surveys consistently report large majorities in favor of repeal.

In the face of such findings, proposals to make the tax system more progressive might seem doomed from the outset. Yet other evidence suggests that reform prospects may be less bleak than they appear. For example, when voters are given even minimal information about the consequences of repeal of the estate tax, their attitudes shift sharply against President Bush's proposal.

According to the Center on Budget and Policy Priorities, for example, repealing the estate tax would reduce federal revenues by close to one trillion dollars during the years between 2012 and 2021. This shortfall would require taking one or more of the following steps: raising income taxes, sales taxes, or other taxes; making further cuts in government services; or increasing the rate at which we borrow from the Chinese, Japanese, and others. Additional borrowing would have to be repaid at market rates of interest, however, so the last option would also entail eventual tax increases or service cuts.

Proponents of tax cuts often insist that the only consequence of lower tax revenue will be reduced government waste. Yet when faced with deep budget deficits, President Bush, who campaigned as an enemy of government waste, proposed deep cuts in services that are not widely regarded as wasteful. For instance, his proposals included a 16 percent reduction in spending for veterans' health care, a 15 percent reduction for education and vocational training, and a 9.6 percent reduction for nutritional assistance for poor mothers with small children. And as noted earlier, his administration made significant cuts in the Energy Department's budget for helping to secure poorly guarded nuclear weapons in the former Soviet Union.

Information matters. In the first of two telephone surveys performed in May 2005, I discovered that when respondents were asked only whether they favored repeal of the estate tax, 74 percent said yes and 26 percent said no. But when a second sample of respondents was given a brief description of the actions necessary to cover the revenue shortfalls caused by repeal, these percentages reversed dramatically. Among informed respondents, 79 percent opposed repeal and only 21 percent favored it.[4]

Income and wealth inequality have been rising sharply in the

United States for several decades, exacting a heavy toll on middle-income families. When market forces cause inequality to grow, public policy in most countries pushes in the opposite direction. That was also once the pattern in the United States. But more recently, we have responded by cutting taxes for the wealthy and reducing services for the needy. Historians will someday struggle to explain this puzzling reversal.

As the economist Herb Stein once famously remarked, if something can't go on forever, it won't. At some point, we will take steps to limit the damage caused by rising disparities in income and wealth. With a push from intelligent political leaders, such steps can be taken sooner rather than later. For even in an age of thirty-second sound bites, American voters have demonstrated their ability to see things from a different angle.

NOTES

1. INTRODUCTION

1. The term *positional good* was first introduced by Fred Hirsch (1976).

2. RECENT CHANGES IN INCOME AND WEALTH INEQUALITY

1. *Wall Street Journal*, May 25, 2005.
2. Ibid.

3. INEQUALITY, HAPPINESS, AND HEALTH

1. For an excellent survey of this literature, see Kahneman, Diener, and Schwartz 1999.
2. Goleman 1996.
3. Davidson 1992.
4. Richard J. Davidson, personal communication.

5. For a more detailed survey of the evidence related to objective correlates of happiness, see Frank 1985: chapter 2.

6. Isen and Levin 1972.

7. As Easterlin (1995) reports in a follow-up study.

8. Smolensky 1965.

9. See Diener et al. 1993.

10. Blanchflower and Oswald 2004.

11. See Diener and Suh 1999.

12. Wilkinson (1996) provides a detailed survey of this literature.

13. For a survey of these studies, see Marmot 1995.

14. Marmot et al. 1978.

15. Marmot et al. 1991.

16. Mazur 1983.

17. Mazur and Lamb 1980.

18. Rose, Bernstein, and Gordon 1975.

19. Wilkinson 1996.

20. Frank and Levine 2005.

21. See, for example, Deaton 2001.

22. Daly, Wilson, and Vasdev 2001.

23. Kennedy, Kawachi, and Prothrow-Stith 1996.

4. ENVY OR CONTEXT?

1. Harry Helson (1964) did the pioneering study on the influence of context on perception.

2. Strack et al. 1990.

3. Smith 1776: chapter 2.

4. Johnson 1998.

5. THE RISING COST OF ADEQUATE

1. Statistics from www.census.gov/prod/2003pubs/02statab/construct .pdf; www.census.gov/hhes/income/histinc/f03.html.

2. Ostvik-White 2003.

3. Bradsher 2002: chapter 9.

4. Gaiter and Brecher 2002.

6. WHY DO WE CARE ABOUT RANK?

1. Frank 1999: chapter 9.

2. Neumark and Postlewaite 1998.

3. See Frank 1984.

7. WHAT TYPES OF CONSUMPTION ARE MOST SENSITIVE TO CONTEXT?

1. Solnick and Hemenway 1998, 2005.

2. Landers, Rebitzer, and Taylor 1996.

3. Carlsson, Johansson-Stenman, and Martinsson 2003.

4. Bowles and Park 2005.

5. These models also predict the observed negative relationship between income inequality and average happiness levels. See Alesina, Di Tella, and McCulloch 2001.

6. Warren and Tyagi 2003.

7. For a more formal description of how this kind of public finance scheme affects spending incentives, see Frank 1996.

8. Heffetz 2004.

9. See Robson 1992.

10. Carlsson, Johansson-Stenman, and Martinsson 2003.

11. Friedman 1957.

12. Bodkin 1959; Liviatan 1963.

13. See, for example, Bernheim, Skinner, and Weinberg 2001.

8. HOW CAN MIDDLE-CLASS FAMILIES AFFORD TO KEEP UP?

1. Statistics from www.bls.gov. For an extended discussion, see Schor 1991.

2. Bowles and Park 2001.

3. Wuthnow 1996.

4. McLeod, Minton, and Curiel 1999.

5. Frank and Levine 2005.

6. Frank and Levine 2005.

7. Curiel, Minton, and McLeod 1999.

8. Frank 2001.

9. See http://tti.tamu.edu/documents/mobility_report_2005.pdf.

10. Frank and Levine 2005.

11. McCoy 2004.

12. Wuthnow 1996: chapter 1.

13. Maas 1998.

14. Loeb and Page 1997.

15. Bok 1993.

16. Van Voorst 1992; Smith and Bush 1997.

17. McGuire 1997.

18. Sjostrum 1997.

19. PR Newswire 1997.

20. Marwick 1997.

21. Copple 1997.

22. Cohen et al. 1996.

9. SMART FOR ONE, DUMB FOR ALL

1. Glass and Singer 1972; Sherrod 1974; Stokols et al. 1978; DeLongis, Folkman, and Lazarus 1988; Koslowsky, Kluger, and Reich 1995.

2. For a detailed survey of the supporting studies, see Frank 1999: chapter 6.

3. Frank 1999: chapter 10.

10. LOOKING AHEAD

1. Frank and Cook 1995.
2. Salkin 2006.

11. LESSONS FOR PUBLIC POLICY

1. For a survey of sumptuary laws and other failed attempts to limit conspicuous consumption, see Frank 1999: chapter 13.

2. For an excellent survey, see Dorris 1996.

3. For a discussion of the so-called flat tax, a form of consumption tax, see Hall and Rabushka 1995. For earlier proposals of a progressive consumption tax, see Fisher and Fisher 1942; Friedman 1943; Kaldor 1955; Bradford 1980; Courant and Gramlich 1984; Seidman 1997; and McCaffrey 2002. Others have defended income taxes with reference to concerns about relative position. See, for example, Hochman and Rogers 1969; Boskin and Sheshinski 1978; and Ireland 1994. Ng (1987) has advocated taxes on specific positional goods.

4. To illustrate, consider a taxpayer whose marginal rate under the current income tax is 0.33, and whose marginal rate under a progressive consumption tax would be 0.70. Under each tax regime, suppose that this taxpayer forgoes an extra dollar of consumption for the length of time it takes for money in a savings account to double in value. How much extra future consumption will his sacrifice support in each case? Under the current income tax, his dollar of forgone consumption generates a bank deposit of $1, which becomes $2 on the date in question. When he withdraws the $2, he must pay $0.33 in income tax on his one dollar of interest income. So $1 of forgone consumption today translates into $1.67 of future consumption under the current income tax. Under the consumption tax, by contrast, forgoing $1 of consumption today would result in a $0.70 reduction in current tax liability, and therefore would support a current bank deposit of $1.70. At withdrawal time, this deposit will have grown to $3.40. To find C_F, the amount of future consumption this deposit will support, we solve $C_F + 0.7C_F = \$3.40$ for $C_F = \$2$. Giving up a dollar of current consumption thus supports only $1.67 of future con-

sumption under the current income tax, but $2 under the progressive consumption tax.

5. Layard 1980: 741.

6. "Losing the Edge" (2005).

7. For surveys of this literature, see Glyn and Milband 1994; and Frank 1999: chapter 15.

12. REFLECTIONS

1. Quoted by Kuczynski (1998).

2. Elgin 1981.

3. Seidman 1997.

4. Frank 2005.

REFERENCES

Ainslie, George. 1992. *Picoeconomics*. New York: Cambridge University Press.

Alesina, Alberto, Rafael Di Tella, and Robert McCulloch. 2001. *Inequality and Happiness: Are Europeans and Americans Different?* CEPR Discussion Paper no. 2877. London: Centre for Economic Policy Research.

Bernheim, B. Douglas, Jonathan Skinner, and Steven Weinberg. 2001. "What Accounts for the Variation in Retirement Wealth among U.S. Households?" *American Economic Review* 91 (September): 832–857.

Blanchflower, David G., and Andrew J. Oswald. 2004. "Well-Being over Time in Britain and the USA." *Journal of Public Economics* 88, nos. 7–8 (July): 1359–1386.

Bodkin, Ronald G. 1959. "Windfall Income and Consumption." *American Economic Review* 49 (September): 602–614.

Bok, Derek. 1993. *The Cost of Talent*. New York: Free Press.

Boskin, Michael, and E. Sheshinski. 1978. "Optimal Redistributive Taxation When Individual Welfare Depends on Relative Income." *Quarterly Journal of Economics* 92: 589–601.

Bowles, Samuel, and Yongjin Park. 2005. "Emulation, Inequality, and

Work Hours: Was Thorstein Veblen Right?" *Economic Journal* 115, no. 507: 397–412.

Bradford, David F. 1980. "The Case for a Personal Consumption Tax." In *What Should Be Taxed?* ed. Joseph Pechman. Washington, DC: Brookings Institution.

Bradsher, Keith. 2002. *High and Mighty*. New York: Public Affairs Books.

Carlsson, Fredrik, Olaf Johansson-Stenman, and Peter Martinsson. 2003. "Do You Enjoy Having More than Others? Survey Evidence of Positional Goods." Goteburg University Working Papers in Economics no. 100, May.

Cohen, Brian A., Richard Wiles, Erik Olson, and Chris Campbell. 1996. "Just Add Water." Report for Natural Resources Defense Fund, Environmental Working Group Online, www.ewg.org, May.

Copple, James. 1997. "Prepared Testimony before the Senate Committee on Labor and Human Resources." *Federal News Service*, April 18.

Courant, Paul, and Edward M. Gramlich. 1984. "The Expenditure Tax: Has the Idea's Time Finally Come?" In *Tax Policy: New Directions and Possibilities*. Washington, DC: Center for National Policy.

Curiel, Jonathan, Torri Minton, and Ramon McLeod. 1999. "Paying with Their Health: Doctors Say Financial Strain Is Making People Sick." *San Francisco Chronicle*, April 14.

Daly, Martin, Margo Wilson, and Shawn Vasdev. 2001. "Income Inequality and Homicide Rates in Canada and the United States." *Canadian Journal of Criminology* 43, no. 2 (April): 219–236.

Davidson, Richard J. 1992. "Anterior Cerebral Asymmetry and the Nature of Emotion." *Brain and Cognition* 6: 245–268.

Deaton, Angus. 2001. "Inequalities in Income and Inequalities in Health." In *The Causes and Consequences of Increasing Inequality*, ed. Finis Welch. Chicago: University of Chicago Press.

DeLongis, Anita, Susan Folkman, and Richard S. Lazarus. 1988. "The Impact of Daily Stress on Health and Mood: Psychological and Social Resources as Mediators." *Journal of Personality and Social Psychology* 54: 486–495.

Diener, Ed, Ed Sandvik, Larry Seidlitz, and Marissa Diener. 1993. "The Relationship between Income and Subjective Well-Being: Relative or Absolute?" *Social Indicators Research* 28: 195–223.

Diener, Ed, and Eunkiik Suh. 1999. "National Differences in Subjective Well-Being." In *Well-Being: The Foundations of Hedonic Psychology*, ed. D. Kahneman, E. Diener, and N. Schwartz. New York: Russell Sage.

Dorris, Gary W. 1996. "Redesigning Regulatory Policy: A Case Study in Urban Smog." PhD dissertation, Cornell University.

Duesenberry, James. 1949. *Income, Saving, and the Theory of Consumer Behavior.* Cambridge, MA: Harvard University Press.

Easterlin, Richard. 1974. "Does Economic Growth Improve the Human Lot?" In *Nations and Households in Economic Growth: Essays in Honor of Moses Abramovitz*, ed. Paul David and Melvin Reder. New York: Academic Press.

———. 1995. "Will Raising the Incomes of All Increase the Happiness of All?" *Journal of Economic Behavior and Organization* 27: 35–47.

Elgin, Duane. 1981. *Voluntary Simplicity.* New York: Morrow.

Fisher, Irving, and Herbert W. Fisher. 1942. *Constructive Income Taxation.* New York: Harper and Brothers.

Frank, Robert H. 1984. "Are Workers Paid Their Marginal Products?" *American Economic Review* 74 (September): 549–571.

———. 1985. *Choosing the Right Pond.* New York: Oxford University Press.

———. 1996. "Consumption Externalities and the Financing of Social Services." In *Individual and Social Responsibility: Child Care, Education, Medical Care, and Long-Term Care in America*, ed. Victor R. Fuchs. National Bureau of Economic Research Conference Report. Chicago: University of Chicago Press.

———. 1999. *Luxury Fever.* New York: Free Press.

———. 2001. "Traffic and Tax Cuts." *New York Times*, May 11.

———. 2005. "The Estate Tax: Efficient, Fair, and Misunderstood." *New York Times*, May 12.

Frank, Robert H., and Philip Cook. 1995. *The Winner-Take-All Society.* New York: Free Press.

Frank, Robert H., and Adam Seth Levine. 2005. "Expenditure Cascades." Cornell University mimeograph.

Friedman, Milton. 1943. "The Tax as a Wartime Measure." *American Economic Review* 33 (March): 50–62.

———. 1957. *A Theory of the Consumption Function.* Princeton, NJ: Princeton University Press.

Gaiter, Dorothy, and John Brecher. 2002. *The Wall Street Journal Guide to Wine, New and Improved: How to Buy, Drink, and Enjoy Wine,* 2nd edition. New York: Broadway.

Galbraith, John Kenneth. 1958. *The Affluent Society.* Boston: Houghton Mifflin.

Glass, D. C., and J. Singer. 1972. *Urban Stressors: Experiments on Noise and Social Stressors.* New York: Academic Press.

Glyn, Andrew, and David Miliband, eds. 1994. *Paying for Inequality: The Economic Cost of Social Injustice.* London: Rivers Oram.

Goleman, Daniel. 1996. "Forget Money; Nothing Can Buy Happiness, Some Researchers Say." *New York Times,* July 16.

Greenstein, Robert, and Isaac Shapiro. 2003. "The New, Definitive CBO Data on Income and Tax Trends." Center on Budget and Policy Priorities, September 23. Posted online at www.cbpp.org/9-23-03tax.htm.

Hall, Robert E., and Alvin Rabushka. 1995. *The Flat Tax,* 2nd edition. Stanford, CA: Hoover Institution.

Heffetz, Ori. 2004. "Conspicuous Consumption and the Visibility of Consumption Expenditures." Princeton University Department of Economics mimeograph.

Helson, Harry. 1964. *Adaptation-Level Theory.* New York: Harper and Row.

Hirsch, Fred. 1976. *Social Limits to Growth.* Cambridge, MA: Harvard University Press.

Hochman, Harold M., and J. D. Rogers. 1969. "Pareto Optimal Redistribution." *American Economic Review* 59: 542–557.

Ireland, Norman. 1994. "On Limiting the Market for Status Signals." *Journal of Public Economics* 53: 91–110.

Isen, A. M., and P. F. Levin. 1972. "Effects of Feeling Good on Helping: Cookies and Kindness." *Journal of Personality and Social Psychology* 21: 384–388.

Johnson, Dirk. 1998. "When Money Is Everything, Except Hers." *New York Times*, October 28.

Kahneman, Daniel, Ed Diener, and Norbert Schwartz, eds. 1999. *Well-Being: The Foundations of Hedonic Psychology*. New York: Russell Sage.

Kaldor, Nicholas. 1955. *An Expenditure Tax*. London: Allen and Unwin.

Kennedy, Bruce P., Ichiro Kawachi, and Deborah Prothrow-Stith. 1996. "Income Distribution and Mortality: Cross Sectional Ecological Study of the Robin Hood Index in the United States." *British Medical Journal* 312: 1004–1007.

Koslowsky, Meni, Avraham N. Kluger, and Mordechai Reich. 1995. *Commuting Stress*. New York: Plenum.

Kuczynski, Alex. 1998. "A Benz for the Wrist." *New York Times*, March 8.

Landers, Renee M., James B. Rebitzer, and Lowell J. Taylor. 1996. "Rat Race Redux: Adverse Selection in the Determination of Work Hours in Law Firms," *American Economic Review* 86: 329–348.

Layard, Richard. 1980. "Human Satisfactions and Public Policy." *Economic Journal* 90: 737–750.

Liviatan, Nissan. 1963. "Tests of the Permanent-Income Hypothesis Based on a Reinterview Savings Survey." In *Measurement in Economics: Studies in Mathematical Economics and Econometrics in Memory of Yehuda Grunfeld*, ed. Carl F. Christ and others. Stanford, CA: Stanford University Press.

Loeb, Susanna, and Marianne E. Page. 1997. "Examining the Link between Wages and Quality in the Teacher Workforce." University of Michigan Department of Economics mimeograph, October.

"Losing the Edge." 2005. *Times of India*, November 17.

Maas, James. 1998. *Power Sleep*. New York: Villard.

Marmot, Michael. 1995. "Social Differentials in Mortality: The Whitehall Studies." In *Adult Mortality in Developed Countries: From Description to Explanation*, ed. Alan D. Lopez, Graziella Casselli, and Tapani Valkonen. New York: Oxford University Press.

Marmot, Michael, G. Rose, M. Shipley, and P. J. S. Hamilton. 1978. "Employment Grade and Coronary Heart Disease." *British Medical Journal* 2: 1109–1112.

Marmot, Michael, George Davey Smith, S. Stanfield, C. Patel, F. North, J. Head, I. White, E. Brunner, and A. Feeney. 1991. "Health Inequalities among British Civil Servants: The Whitehall II Study." *Lancet* 337: 1387–1393.

Marwick, Charles. 1997. "Putting Money Where the U.S. Mouth Is: Initiative on Food Safety Gets Under Way." *Journal of the American Medical Association* 277, no. 17 (May 7): 1340–1343.

Mazur, Allan. 1983. "Physiology, Dominance, and Aggression in Humans." In *Prevention and Control of Aggression*, ed. A. Goldstein. New York: Pergamon.

Mazur, Allan, and T. Lamb. 1980. "Testosterone, Status, and Mood in Human Males." *Hormones and Behavior* 14: 236–246.

McCaffrey, Ed. 2002. *Fair, Not Flat*. Chicago: University of Chicago Press.

McCoy, Krisha. 2004. "Sleeping Less Than Eight Hours a Night May Stimulate Your Appetite." Women and Infants' Hospital of Rhode Island, www.womenandinfants.com/body.cfm?id = 388&chunkiid = 88476.

McGuire, Mark. 1997. "A Rumble and Everything Went." *Albany Times Union*, March 30.

McLeod, Ramon, Torri Minton, and Jonathon Curiel. 1999. "Making More, Having Less: Bay Area Families Struggle to Earn Middle-Class Status." *San Francisco Chronicle*, April 13.

Neumark, David, and Andrew Postlewaite. 1998. "Relative Income Concerns and the Rise in Married Women's Employment." *Journal of Public Economics* 70: 157–183.

Ng, Yew-Kwang. 1987. "Diamonds Are a Government's Best Friend: Burden-Free Taxes on Goods Valued for Their Values." *American Economic Review* 77: 186–191.

Ostvik-White, Bjornulf. 2003. "Income Inequality and Median House Prices in 200 School Districts." Masters thesis, Cornell University Institute of Public Policy.

PR Newswire. 1997. "Oakland Road Commissioners Divert Money for 'Pothole Emergency.'" April 19.

Robson, Arthur. 1992. "Status, the Distribution of Wealth, Private and Social Attitudes to Risk." *Econometrica* 60: 837–857.

Rose, R., I. Bernstein, and T. Gordon. 1975. "Consequences of Social Conflict on Plasma Testosterone Levels in Rhesus Monkeys." *Psychosomatic Medicine* 37: 50–61.

Salkin, Allen. 2006. "Pimp My Grill." *New York Times*, May 28.

Schor, Juliet. 1991. *The Overworked American*. New York: Basic Books.

Seidman, Laurence. 1997. *The USA Tax: A Progressive Consumption Tax*. Cambridge, MA: MIT Press.

Sherrod, D. R. 1974. "Crowding, Perceived Control, and Behavioral Aftereffects." *Journal of Applied Social Psychology* 4: 171–186.

Sjostrom, Joseph. 1997. "Projects' Delays Add to Expense Down Road; Stalled Projects Just Speed Deterioration of Crumbling Highways." *Chicago Tribune*, July 31.

Smith, Adam. 1776. *The Wealth of Nations*. Online edition, posted at www.online-literature.com/adam_smith/wealth_nations/.

Smith, Robert L., and Robert J. Bush. 1997. "A Qualitative Evaluation of the US Timber Bridge Market." *Forest Products Journal* 47, no. 1 (January): 37–42.

Smolensky, Eugene. 1965. "The Past and Present Poor." In *The Concept of Poverty*, by Task Force on Economic Growth and Opportunity. Washington, DC: Chamber of Commerce of the United States.

Solnick, Sara J., and David Hemenway. 1998. "Is More Always Better?" *Journal of Economic Behavior and Organization* 37, no. 3: 373–383.

———. 2005. "Are Positional Concerns Stronger in Some Domains Than in Others?" *American Economic Review* 95, no. 2 (May): 147–151.

Stokols, Daniel, Raymond W. Novaco, Jeannette Stokols, and Joan Campbell. 1978. "Traffic Congestion, Type A Behavior, and Stress." *Journal of Applied Psychology* 63: 467–480.

Strack, Fritz, N. Schwarz, B. Chassein, D. Kern, and D. Wagner. 1990. "The Salience of Comparison Standards and the Activation of Social Norms: Consequences for Judgments of Happiness and Their Communication." *British Journal of Social Psychology* 29 (December): 303–314.

Van Voorst, Bruce. 1992. "Why America Has So Many Potholes." *Time*, May 4, pp. 64–65.

Veenhoven, Ruut. 1993. *Happiness in Nations: Subjective Appreciation of Life in 56 Nations*. Rotterdam: Erasmus University.

Warren, Elizabeth, and Amelia Warren Tyagi. 2003. *The Two-Income Trap: Why Middle-Class Mothers and Fathers Are Going Broke*. New York: Basic Books.

Wilkinson, Richard G. 1996. *Unhealthy Societies: The Afflictions of Inequality*. London: Routledge.

Wolff, Edward. 1998. "Recent Trends in Wealth Ownership." Paper for the Conference on Benefits and Mechanisms for Spreading Asset Ownership in the United States, New York University, December.

Wuthnow, Robert. 1996. *Poor Richard's Principle: Rediscovering the American Dream through the Moral Dimension of Work, Business, and Money*. Princeton, NJ: Princeton University Press.

INDEX

Note: Page references in italics indicate illustrations.

Text: 10/15 Janson

Display: Janson

Compositor: BookMatters, Berkeley

Indexer: Carol Roberts

Printer and binder: Thomson-Shore, Inc.